GW01236601

Published in 2023 by Hardie Grant Explore, an imprint of
Hardie Grant Publishing

Hardie Grant Explore (Melbourne)
Wurundjeri Country
Building 1, 658 Church Street
Richmond, Victoria 3121

Hardie Grant Explore (Sydney)
Gadigal Country
Level 7, 45 Jones Street
Ultimo, NSW 2007

www.hardiegrant.com/au/explore

All rights reserved. No part of this publication may be reproduced, stored in a retrieval system or transmitted in any form by any means, electronic, mechanical, photocopying, recording or otherwise, without the prior written permission of the publishers and copyright holders.

The moral rights of the author have been asserted.

Copyright English text © Karungkarni Art & Culture Aboriginal Corporation on behalf of the Gurindji community, and Scale Free Network, 2023
Copyright Gurindji and Gurindji Kriol text © Karungkarni Art & Culture Aboriginal Corporation on behalf of the Gurindji community, 2023
Copyright concept and design © Hardie Grant Publishing 2023

A catalogue record for this book is available from the National Library of Australia

Hardie Grant acknowledges the Traditional Owners of the Country on which we work, the Wurundjeri People of the Kulin Nation and the Gadigal People of the Eora Nation, and recognises their continuing connection to the land, waters and culture. We pay our respects to their Elders past and present.

Cover artwork by Mary Smiler and Lucy Tanami.
Endpaper artwork *Two Way* by Topsy Dodd Ngarnjal

Tamarra
ISBN 9781741178302

10 9 8 7 6 5 4 3 2

Publisher
Melissa Kayser
Project editor
Amanda Louey
Editor
Irma Gold
Proofreader
Jenny Varghese
Design
Keisha Leon
Typesetting
Kerry Cooke
Production coordinator
Simone Wall

Image credits
p. 2: map/Brenda Thornley; p. 4 (left): Pk_camera/Shutterstock.com, (right), 33, 52: Peter Waters/Dreamstime.com; p. 5: Claus Lunau/Science Photo Library; p. 8, 68, 72, 74: Penny Smith; p. 11, 12, 15, 16, 20, 23, 26, 29, 30, 76, 78, 79 (left & top): Briony Barr; p. 19, 60, 77: Brenda L Croft; p. 36: Gregory Dimijian/Science Photo Library; p. 39: Melvyn Yeo/Science Photo Library; p. 40: Gregory Crocetti; p. 43: Ruben Duro/Science Photo Library; p. 44: Kurt Orion G; p. 47: Nicolas Reusens/Science Photo Library; p. 48: Lirtlon/Dreamstime.com; p. 55: Jared Leadbetter; p. 56: Vinicius R. Souza/Shutterstock.com; p. 63: CSIRO; p. 64: Mike Gillam; p. 67: Aroona Kavathekar/Alamy Stock Photo; p. 75 (top): B. Manning, (bottom): Susannah Tosh; p. 79 (right): Karungkarni Art; All artworks photographed by Mick Richards.

Colour reproduction by Splitting Image Colour Studio

Printed and bound in China by LEO Paper Products LTD.

The paper this book is printed on is certified against the Forest Stewardship Council® Standards and other sources. FSC® promotes environmentally responsible, socially beneficial and economically viable management of the world's forests.

TAMARRA
A STORY OF TERMITES ON GURINDJI COUNTRY

WORDS

Violet Wadrill
Topsy Dodd Ngarnjal
Leah Leaman

Cecelia Edwards
Cassandra Algy

Felicity Meakins
Briony Barr
Gregory Crocetti

ARTWORK AND PHOTOGRAPHY

Topsy Dodd Ngarnjal
Violet Wadrill
Rosemary Johnson
Serena Donald
Leah Leaman
Pauline Ryan
Margaret Winbye
Magdalene Winbye
Roberta Winbye

Mary Smiler
Rosie Smiler
Joanne Stevens
Rachel Rennie
Lucy Tanami
Cassandra Algy
Caroline Jimmy
Martina Mandijerry
Cecelia Edwards

Sophia Donnelly-Patterson
Tara Long
Merrilyn Frith
Narelle Morris
Theresa Yibwoin
Brenda L Croft
Briony Barr
Penny Smith
Kalkaringi School Students

ABOUT THIS BOOK

Gurindji Country is located 800 kilometres south-west of Darwin in the Northern Territory. Look at the map to see where it is in Australia.

'Tamarra' means 'termite mound' in Gurindji. When spoken, the 't' sounds more like a 'd' and the 'rr' is rolled (similar to a Scottish 'r'), so it sounds a bit like 'DAH-mah-rrah'.

Languages in this book

This story uses three different languages. The **Gurindji**, **Gurindji Kriol** and **English** words are colour-coded. Gurindji is used for traditional knowledge and Gurindji Kriol is used for non-Indigenous knowledge.

Learn more about Gurindji languages on page 76.

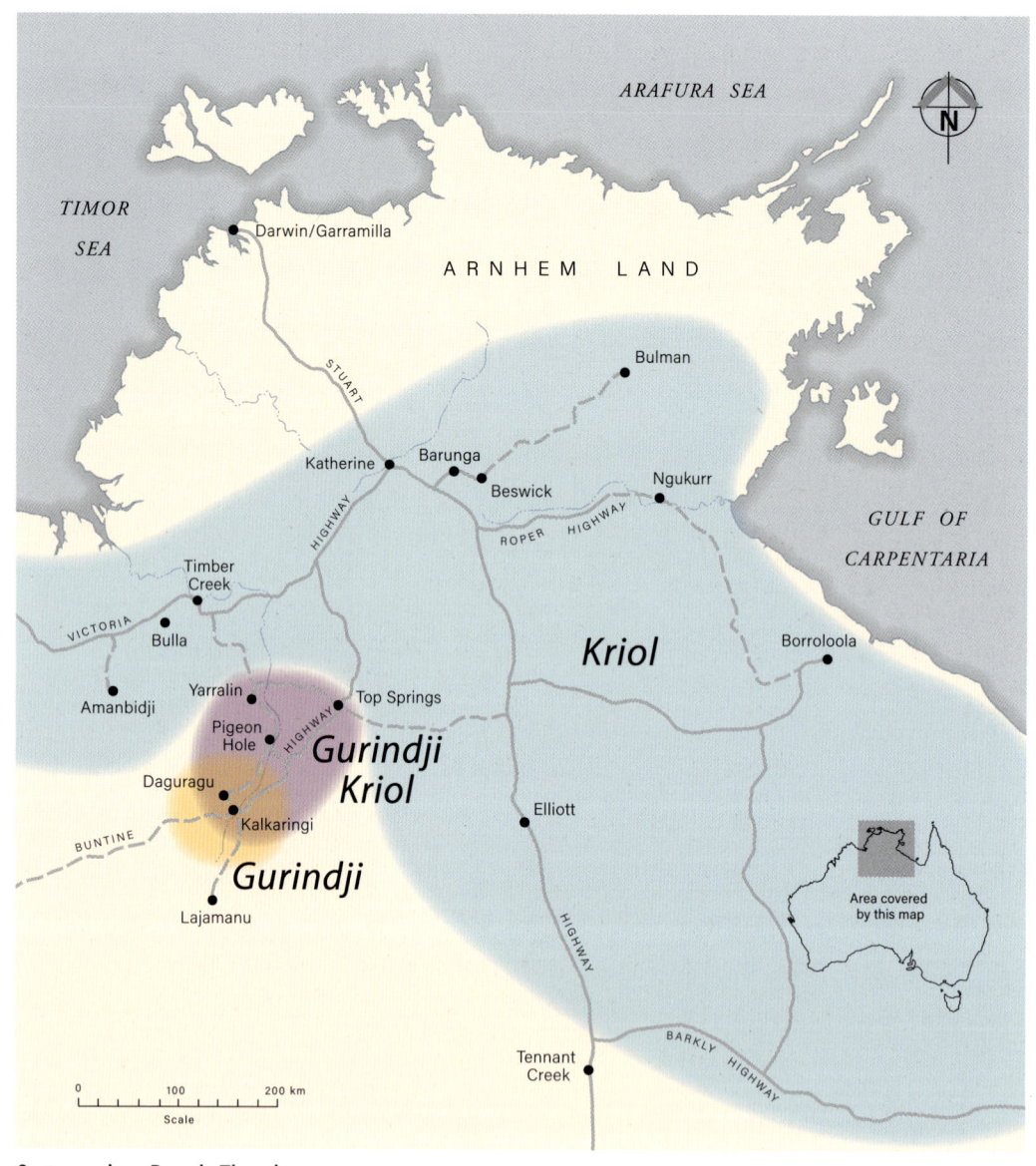

Cartographer: Brenda Thornley

Aboriginal and Torres Strait Islander Peoples are advised that this publication may contain the names and images of deceased people. Hardie Grant apologises for any distress this may inadvertently cause.

Glossary

Here are some Gurindji words that you might like to learn yourself. While reading this book, you'll see a key glossary word for that page coloured blue.

Gurindji	Pronunciation	English
jaju	JAH-ju	maternal grandmother
janyja	JUN-jah	ground
jimpiri	JIM-bi-ri	hole, tunnel
jungkuwurru	JUNG-gu-wu-du	echidna
jurlaka	JU-la-gah	bird
juru	JU-ru	nest, termite nursery
kampij	GUM-bij	egg
kapuku	KAH-bu-ku	sister
karu	KAH-ru	child, baby
kawarla	KAU-wa-lah	coolamon (large wooden dish)
kirri	GI-di	woman
kupuwupu	KU-buu-bu	lemongrass
kurrurij	GU-du-ridge	car
lampura	LAM-bu-rah	axe
majul	MAH-jul	belly, tummy, gut
manyanyi	MAH-nyan-nyi	a type of small bush
marlarn	MAH-lan	river red gum
munkurt	MUN-gut	termite

Gurindji	Pronunciation	English
ngamayi	NGAH-may	mother
ngarlaka	NGAH-la-gah	head
ngawa	NGAU-wah	water, rain
ngirirri	NGI-ri-di	hakea (a type of plant)
ngurra	NGU-dah	Country, home
pingi	BING-i	ant
pinka	BIN-gah	river
pirna	BIN-ah	winged termite
tamarra	DAH-mah-rrah	termite mound
tingarri	DING-ah-rri	knee
tiwuwaji	DI-wu-wah-ji	winged termite
waringarri	WAH-ri-nga-di	defender (termite)
warlu	WAH-lu	fire, firewood
warrwa	WAHRR-wah	spinifex
wartan	WAH-dahn	hand
warukkaji	WAH-ruk-ga-ji	worker (termite)
wulngarn	WUL-ngan	sun
wurrumu	WU-du-mu	road

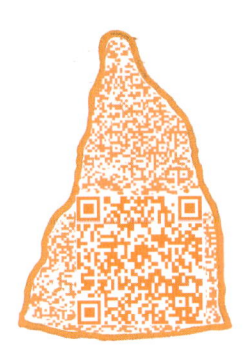

This termite mound is a QR code. Scan it to hear the story in Gurindji (spoken by Violet Wadrill) or Gurindji Kriol (spoken by Cecelia Edwards and Cassandra Algy). You can also listen to the glossary words.

TERMITES

The main termites on Gurindji Country are called spinifex termites. There are five types:
- Mother (queen): lays all the eggs
- Father (king): helps protect the mother
- Defenders (soldiers): protect the workers, the queen and the termite mound
- Workers: collect food and water, build the mound, dig the tunnels, feed and clean the entire family
- Winged termites: future mothers and fathers in new termite mounds

Winged termites in flight

Worker termite

Like all insects, termites have six legs and three body parts (a head, thorax and abdomen). Most insects have a hard exoskeleton, which is like a suit of armour to protect their body. But termites have a soft exoskeleton, which makes it easier for predators, especially ants, to hurt them.

Worker termites: inside and out

Antennae can sense smells, touch, moisture and air movement.

Termites have a pair of claws for gripping mound walls and climbing blades of grass.

Spiracles are small breathing holes that all insects have down the side of their abdomen for oxygen to come in and carbon dioxide to go out.

Small glands called cerci are stroked by other termites to request food (in the form of poo!).

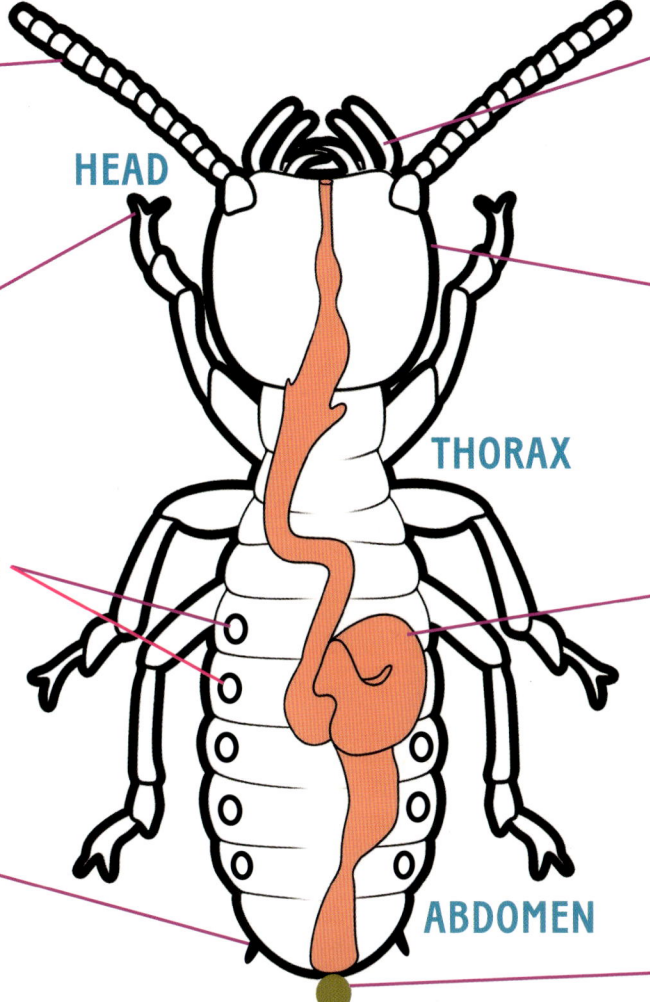

HEAD

THORAX

ABDOMEN

Worker termites have jaws of steel to cut through hard pieces of spinifex grass.

Worker termites use their cheeks to carry water collected from underground.

The hindgut of worker termites holds lots of different bacteria, which helps them convert plants into energy and food.

Termites share leftover nutrients by feeding other termites their poo!

ALL ABOUT POO!

Worker termites do different types of poo:
- Baby food poo is very soft poo for young babies and the mother termite (queen).
- Regular food poo is partly digested poo for older babies and defenders (soldiers).
- Poo glue is used on pieces of sand and clay for building.
- Leftover poo isn't wasted. It is stored in the walls of the mound to help keep it cool.

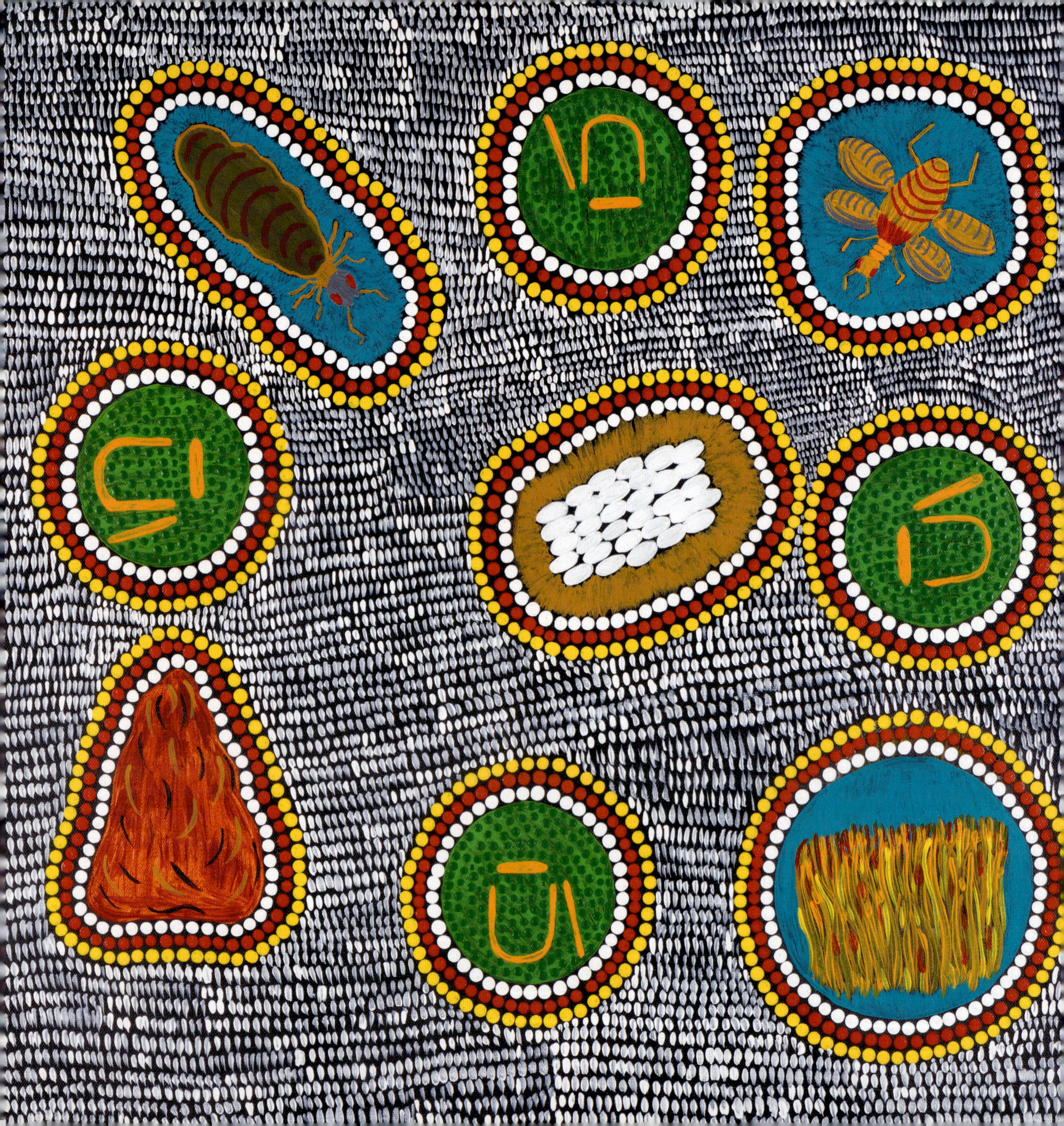

KARU

BABY

Artist: Serena Donald

Wijkuparri Daguragu-la, karu ngu paraj punya. Nyanuny-ju jaju-ngku karu-ma punyuk manana. Nyanuny-ju jaju-ngku tamarra-lu kamparnana puya-ngka. Kirri-walija ngulu partaj yanana kururij-ja tamarra ngirirri nyampa puntanup ngulu manana karu-wu kamparnup-ku.

On Gurindji Country in the town of Daguragu, a baby is born.
To make them strong, grandmother will treat the child's body with termite mound.
The women jump into a car to gather ingredients for the ritual.

DID YOU KNOW?

All Gurindji babies go through a bush medicine treatment called karu kamparnup. Termite mound (called tamarra) is an important ingredient.

- Gurindji
- English
- Glossary word

Artists (pp. 9, 10, 13, 14, 80–81): Briony Barr, Merrilyn Frith, Caroline Jimmy, Martina Mandijerry, Penny Smith, Joanne Stevens, Lucy Tanami, Margaret Winbye, Magdalene Winbye and Roberta Winbye.

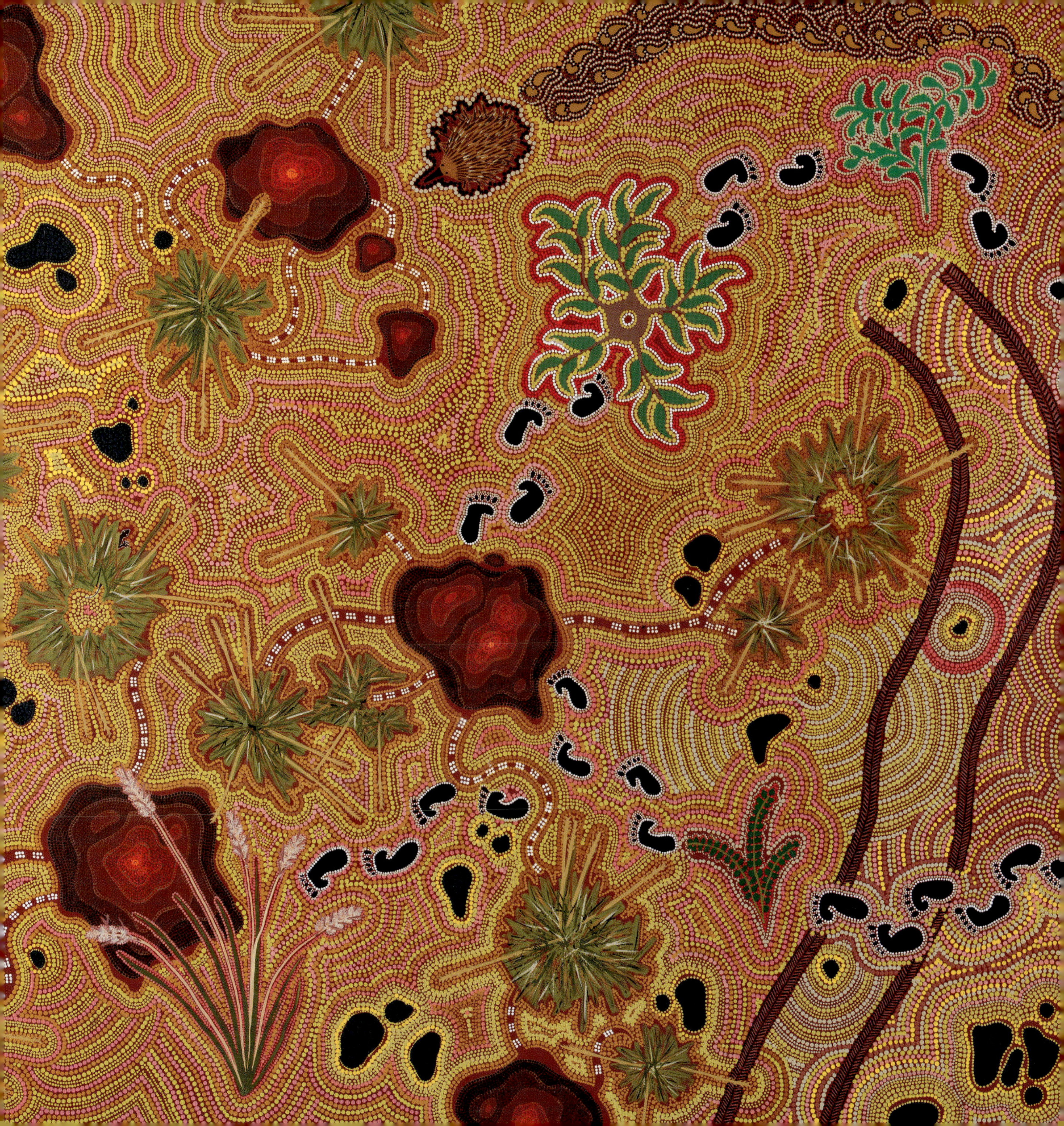

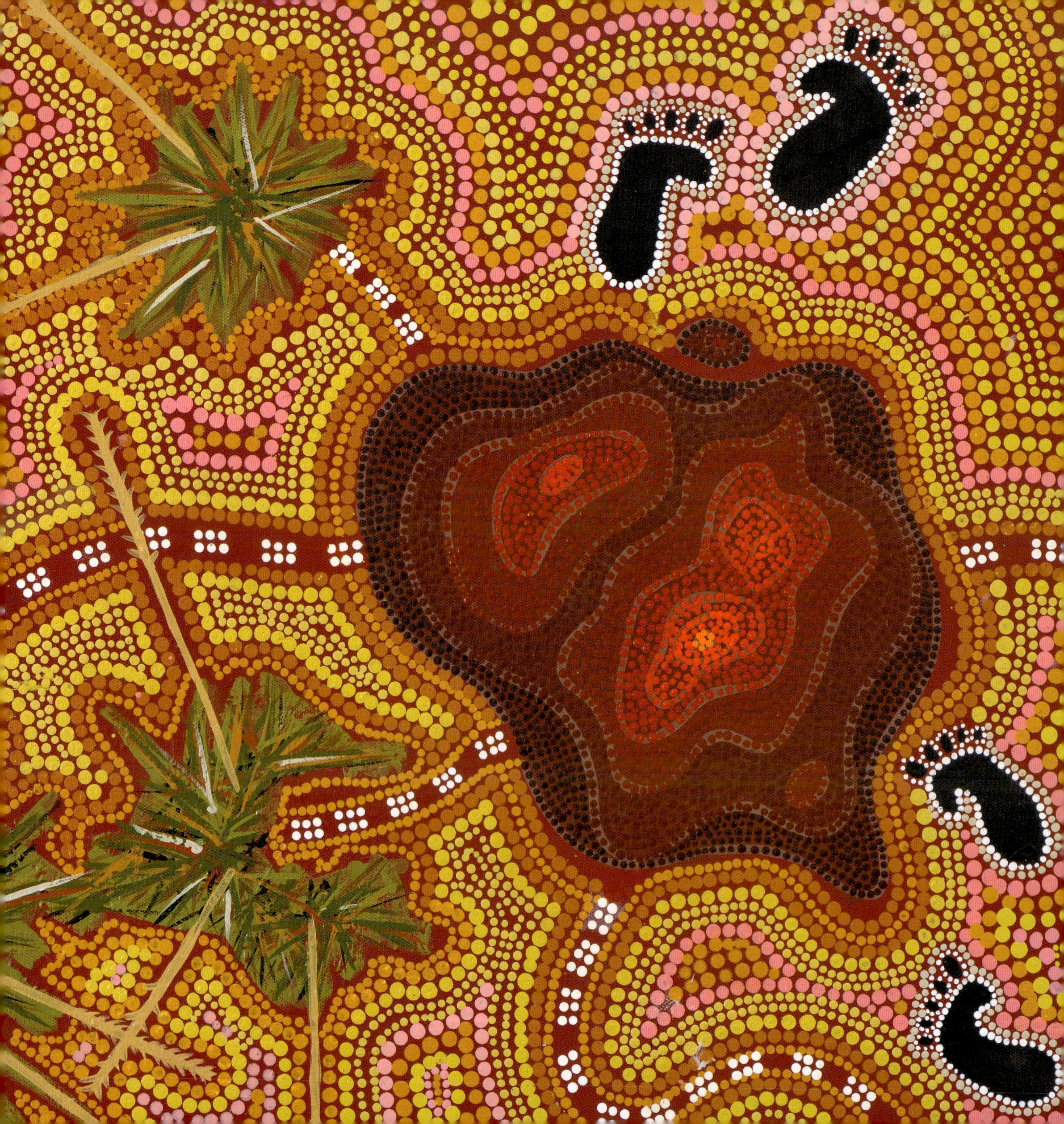

Kirri-walija kalu ngulu yanana warrwa-ngka. Tuturrp nguyina warrwa-ngku pungana. Kirri-ngku-ma jintaku-lu-ma lampura warrkuj mani. Kirri-ngku palyjirrp panana lampura-yawung-kulu-ma tamarra.

As the women walk between clumps of spinifex, the leaves spike their legs. One woman takes an axe and breaks off a piece of termite mound.

DID YOU KNOW?

Spinifex is one of the strongest plants in the world! When Gurindji People make traditional axes, they attach the head with a strong glue made from the spinifex plant and then tie it tight using strings of kangaroo tendon.

Gurindji · English · Glossary word

**Kirtkirt manana ngulu kirri-walija-lu-ma ngirirri.
Yapayapa manyanyi ngulu tuptup manana wurrumu-la.
Punyu ngapuk ngulu manana manyanyi.**

The women break off the dry branches of a ngirirri tree.
They pluck what they need from the manyanyi plant growing near the road, passing the leaves around to smell the fragrance.

DID YOU KNOW?

First Nations women have been collecting plants to make bush medicines for more than 60,000 years. Gurindji women often describe their Country as a chemist. It has everything needed to make bodies strong and healthy.

Gurindji English Glossary word

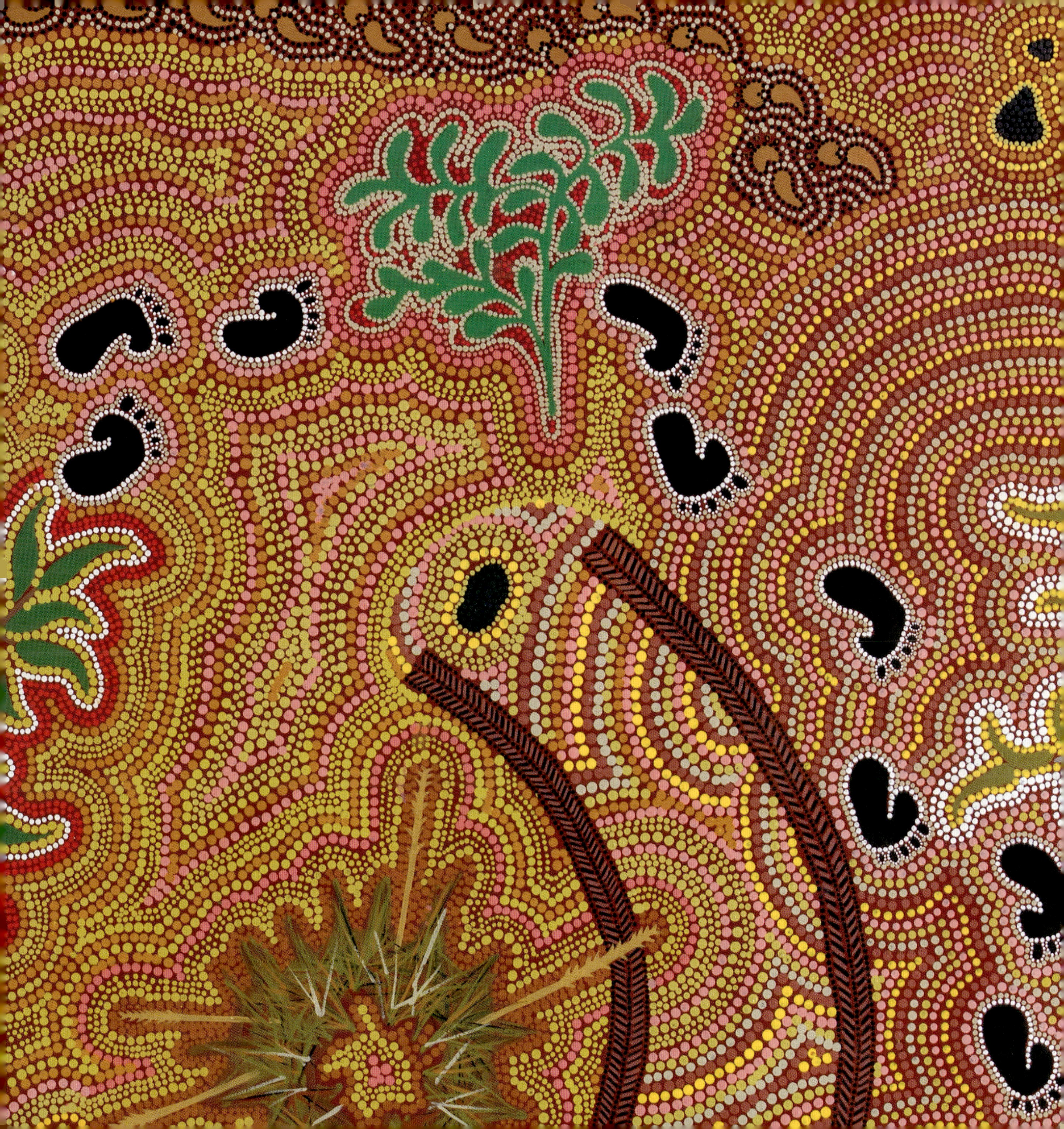

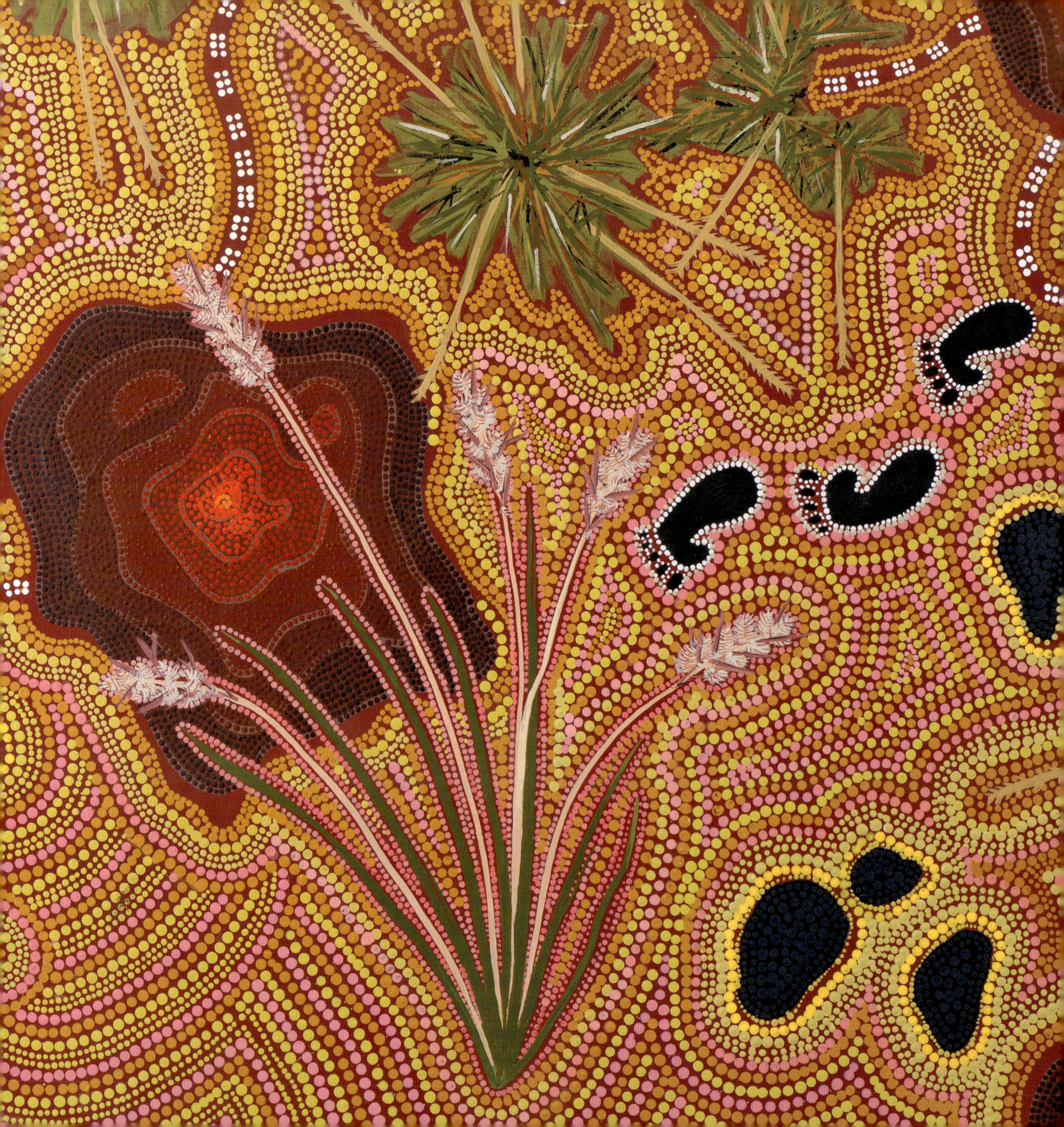

Yalanginyi-ma yirrikaji
ngulu paraj punya
kupuwupu-purrupurru,
ngulu paraj punya.
Warlu ngulu pirrkap
manana yalangka.
Karu ngulu kangana
pinka-kurra murlangkurra.

After the women find
the yirrijkaji plants
and lemongrass,
it's time to prepare the fire,
and bring the baby
down to the river.

DID YOU KNOW?

Kupuwupu is a native lemongrass that is used as medicine. When Gurindji People have a cold, they bathe in kupuwupu or drink it as a tea. It smells and tastes delicious!

Gurindji   English   Glossary word

Lurlu ngulu karrinyana janyja-ka kirri-walija-ma. Tamarra ngulu kirtkirt manana. Warlu-ngka ngulu yuwanana. Kalypak ngulu panana tamarra tajkarra. Ngawa-ngka ngulu japurr yuwanana.

The women sit on the ground. Grandmother breaks the termite mound into pieces and places them on the fire. When the mound is cooked, she crushes it with water in a bowl.

Gurindji · English · Glossary word

DID YOU KNOW?

Gurindji grandmothers usually perform this special process on their grandchildren and, because of this, the baby takes on some of the grandmother's personality. Are you like your grandmother?

Artist: Tara Long

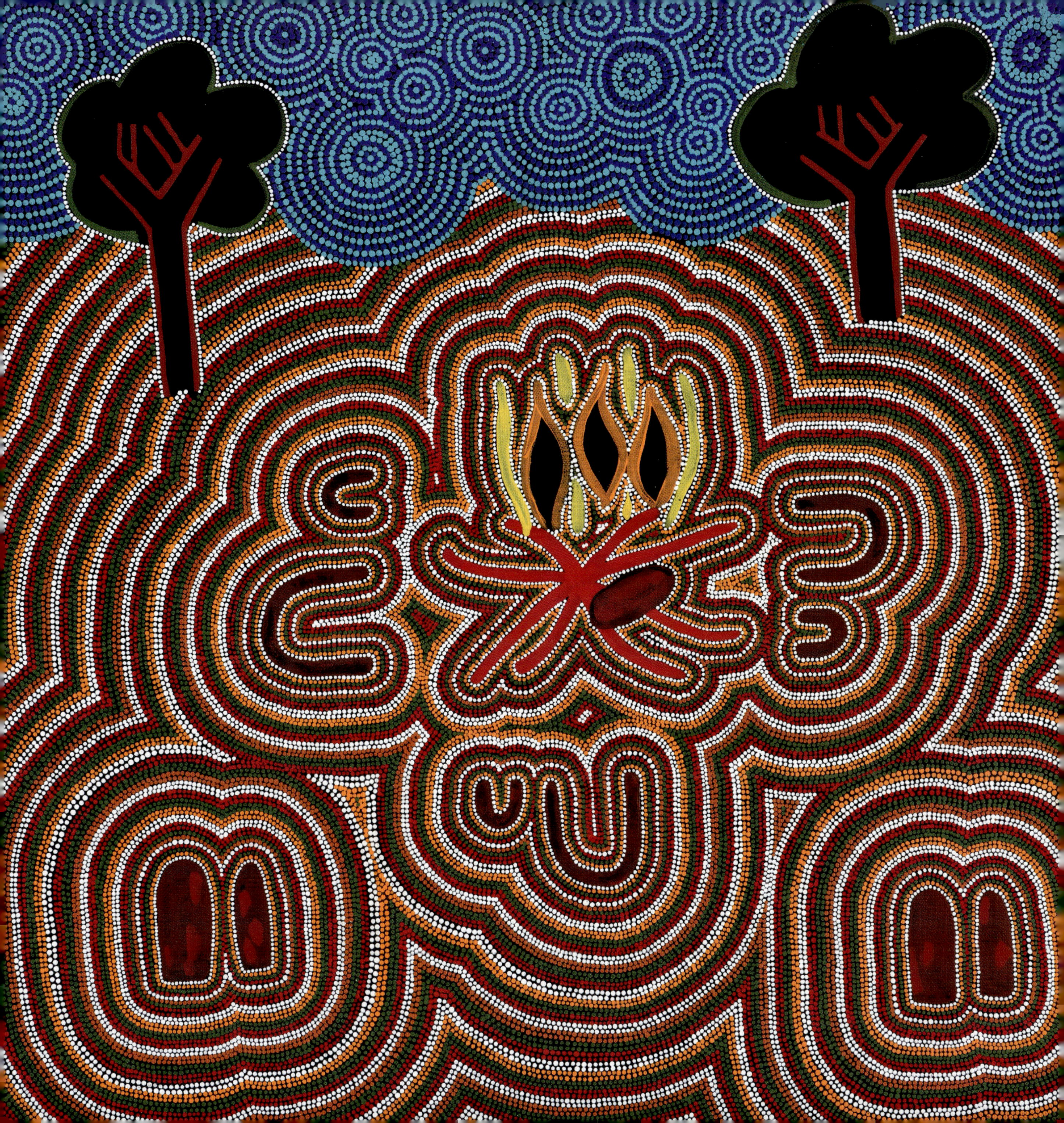

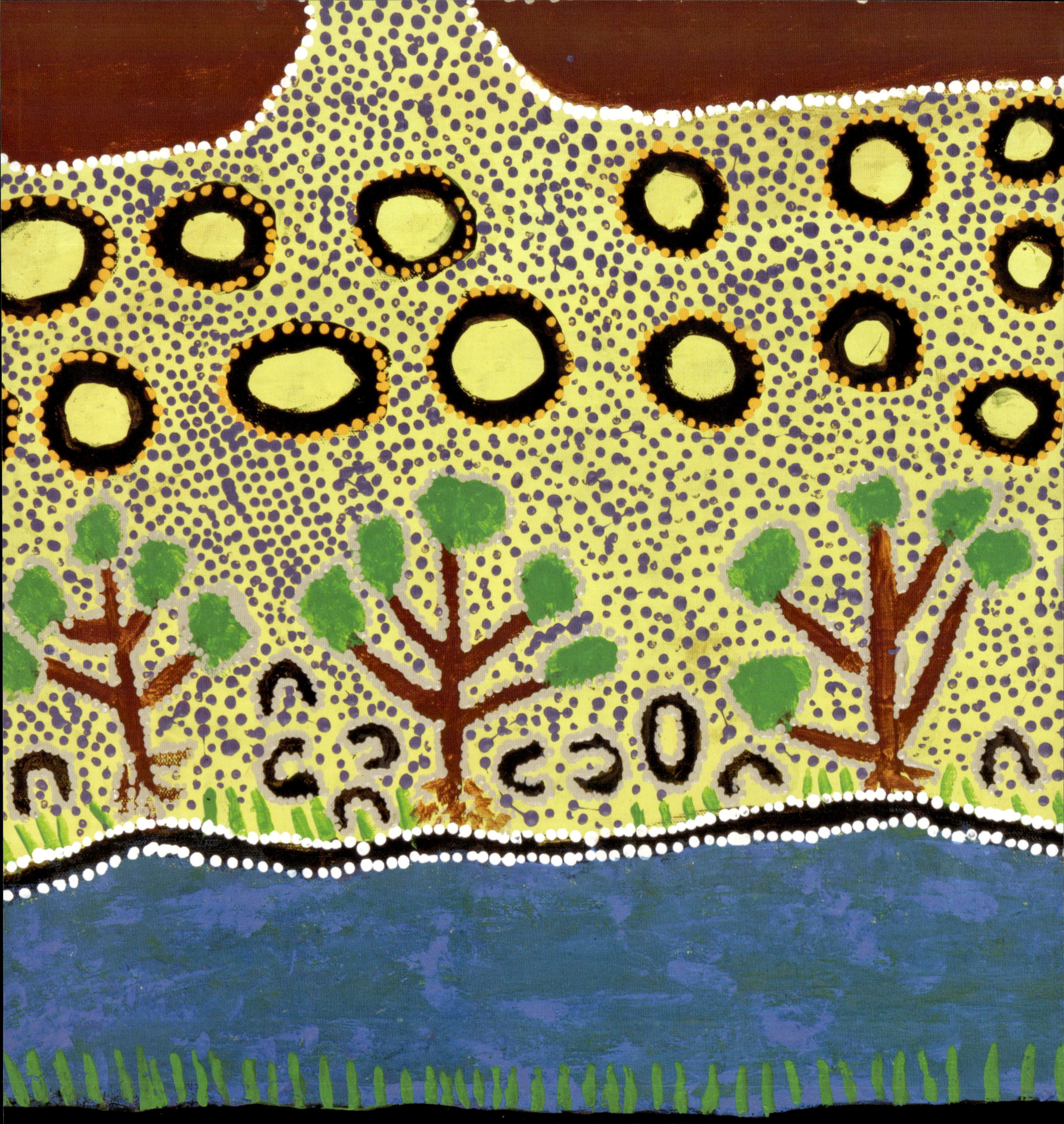

**Turrku ngulu manana karu-ma kankula-piya.
Tupurrung ngurla kanyjuliyit-nganang yanana.
Ngapuk manana karu-ngku-ma yalungku-ma kanyjuliyit.**

The women hold the baby over the steam rising from the bowl.
The warmth surrounds their body, and the baby inhales the vapours.

DID YOU KNOW?

Gurindji women warm leaves from a gum tree called marlarn and sprinkle water onto them to create a gentle, white smoke. Babies, as well as older children and adults, are bathed in a healing smoke which helps strengthen the body and connections with family and Country.

Gurindji · English · Glossary word

Artist: Theresa Yibwoin

Jalyi-ngka ngulu karu makin yuwanana. Kuya-ngka ngulu yuwanana tamarra-ma tingarri-la majul-a puya-ngka ngarlaka-la. Kukijkarra ngulu-rla tamarra jayingana wartan-tu.

The women lay the baby on a soft bed of leaves. Their loving hands cover the baby's knees, head, body and belly in the warm, brown paste. Grandmother gently gives the baby some of the mix to drink.

DID YOU KNOW?

Warm termite mound paste is used to strengthen a baby's body and spirit. It can also be used on a mother's breasts to help milk flow.

Gurindji   English   Glossary word

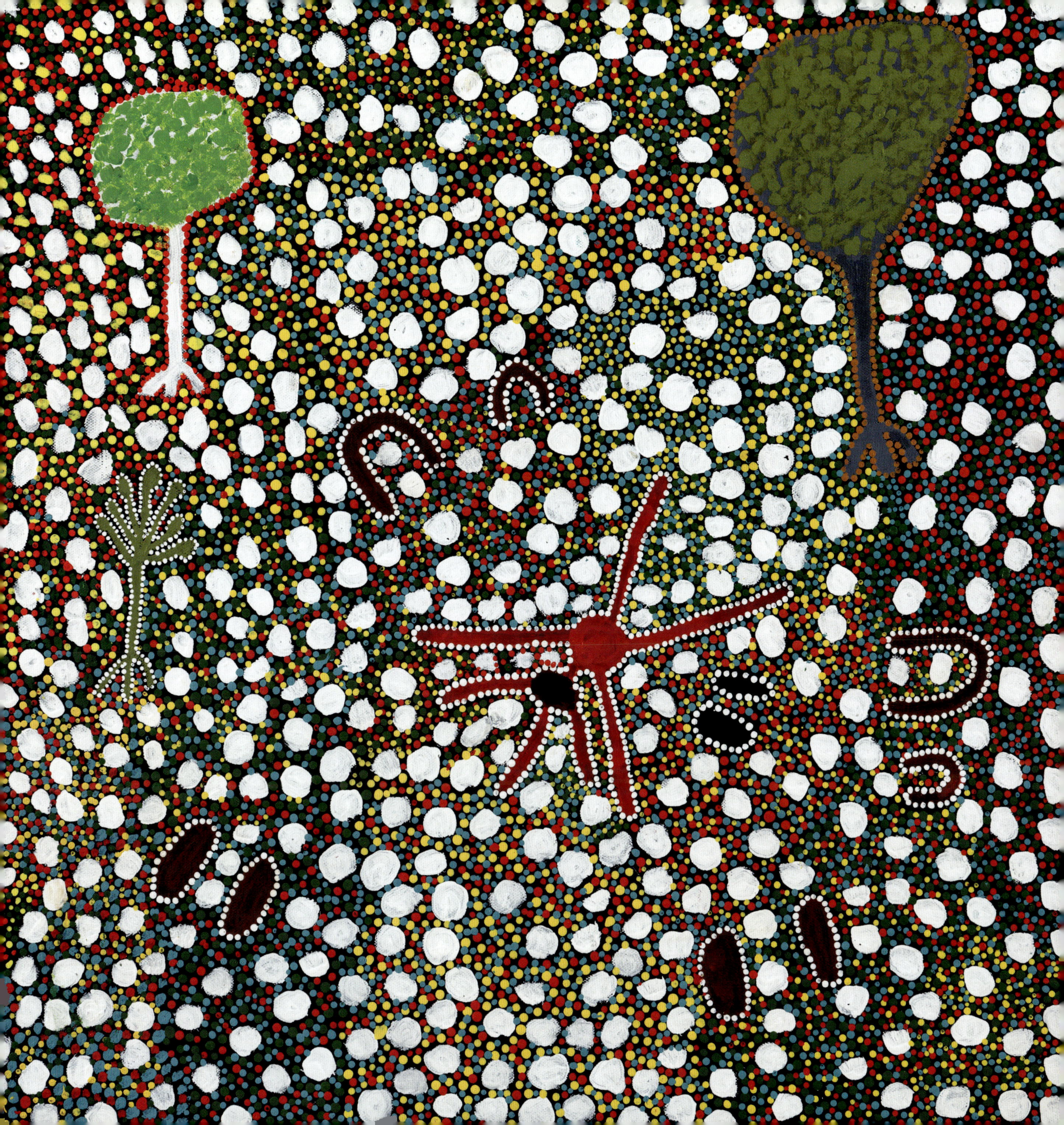

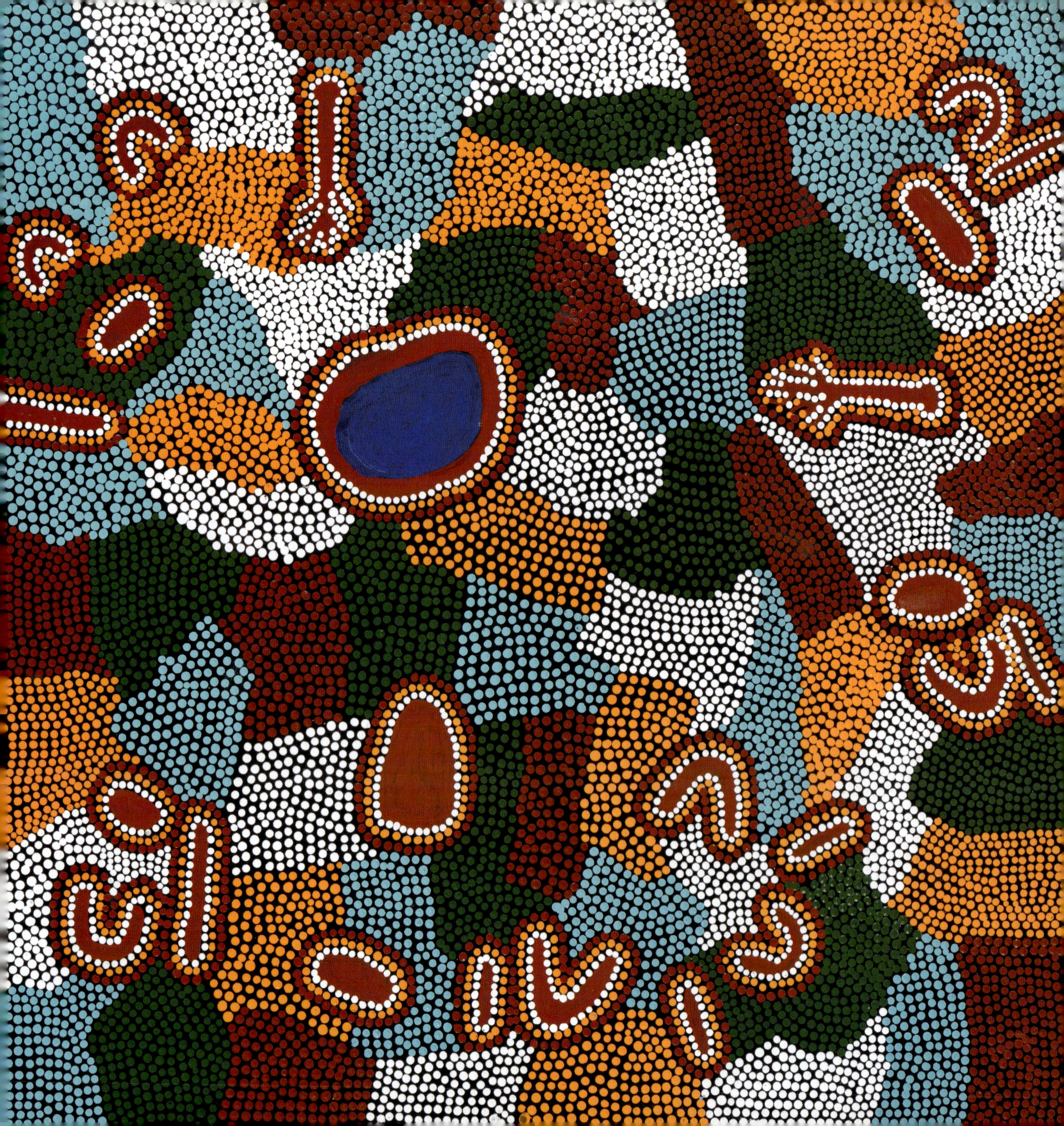

Makin karrinyana punyuk tamarra-nginyi kamparnup-nginyi mum-kula. Kaputkaput tarukap yuwanana ngamayi-lu-ma kilkak karu-ma tamarra-nginyi-ma. Punyu na ngu karru kamparnup-nginyi ngarlaka, ngamany. Wumpulungkarraaji mingipkaji, kalurirrpkaji karu-ma nyila-ma na karru.

Left overnight, the minerals will have time to soak in. Tomorrow morning, the mother will wash the baby's skin clean. The soft spot in the child's skull will close, and soon they'll be able to roll, crawl and walk.

DID YOU KNOW?

When babies are born they have a soft spot on the top of their head called a ngamany (fontenelle). Gurindji People use warm termite mound paste to help new babies grow strong skulls.

Gurindji · English · Glossary word

Artist: Violet Wadrill

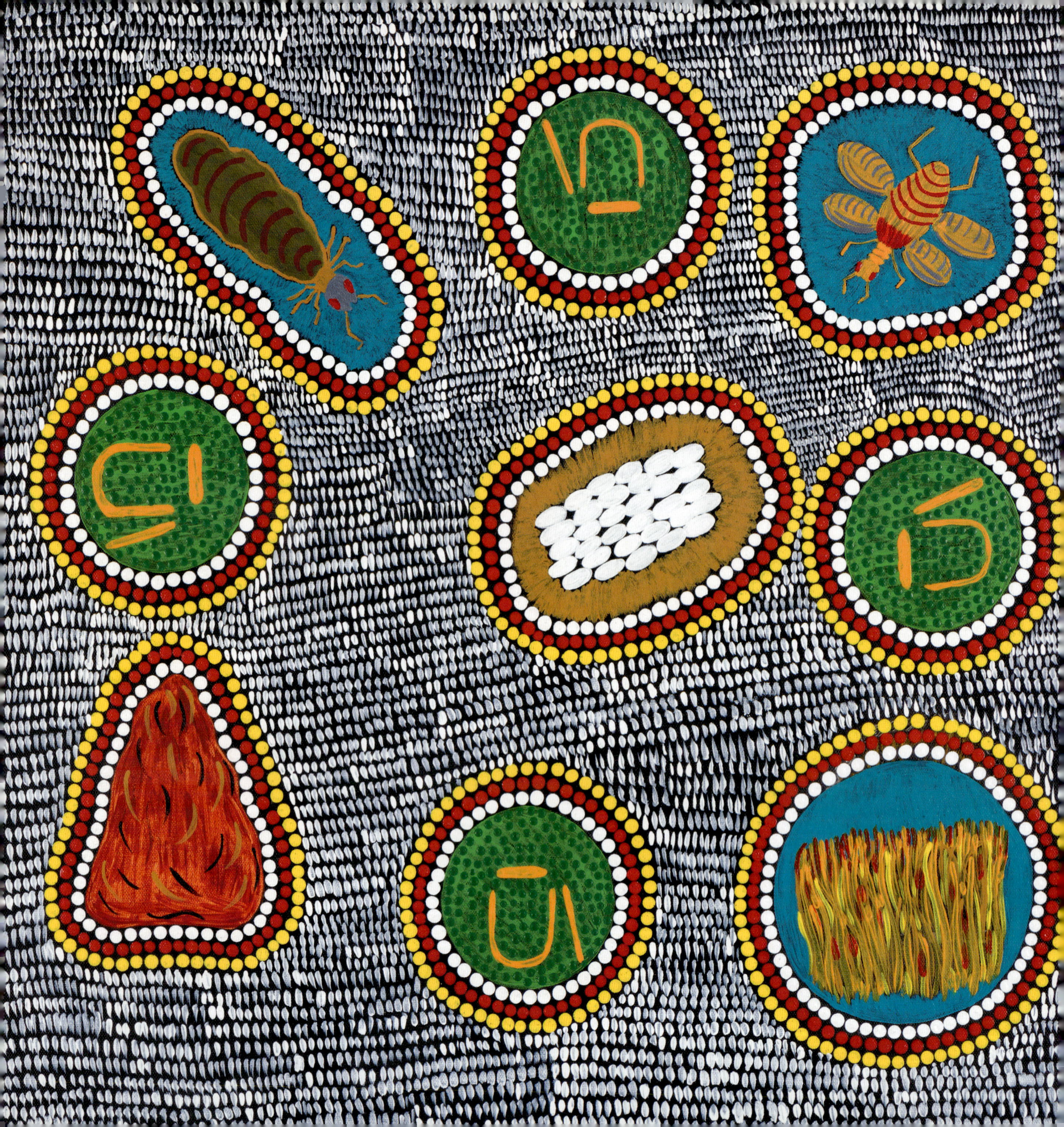

WARRWA

SPINIFEX

Artist: Serena Donald

Wulngarn-tu im barnim kanyjurrak nyawa Gurindji Kantri. Kulojap kawirri-ngka manyjamanyja-ngka, dei grouimap warrwa-walija.

The sun beats down on Gurindji Country. Close to the rusty-red earth, among the wattle and gum trees, grows the spinifex grass.

DID YOU KNOW?

On Gurindji Country, the skies are huge and blue. The earth is a rusty-red colour because it is full of iron. The Victoria River runs through this Country.

Gurindji Kriol · English · Glossary word

Artist: Leah Leaman

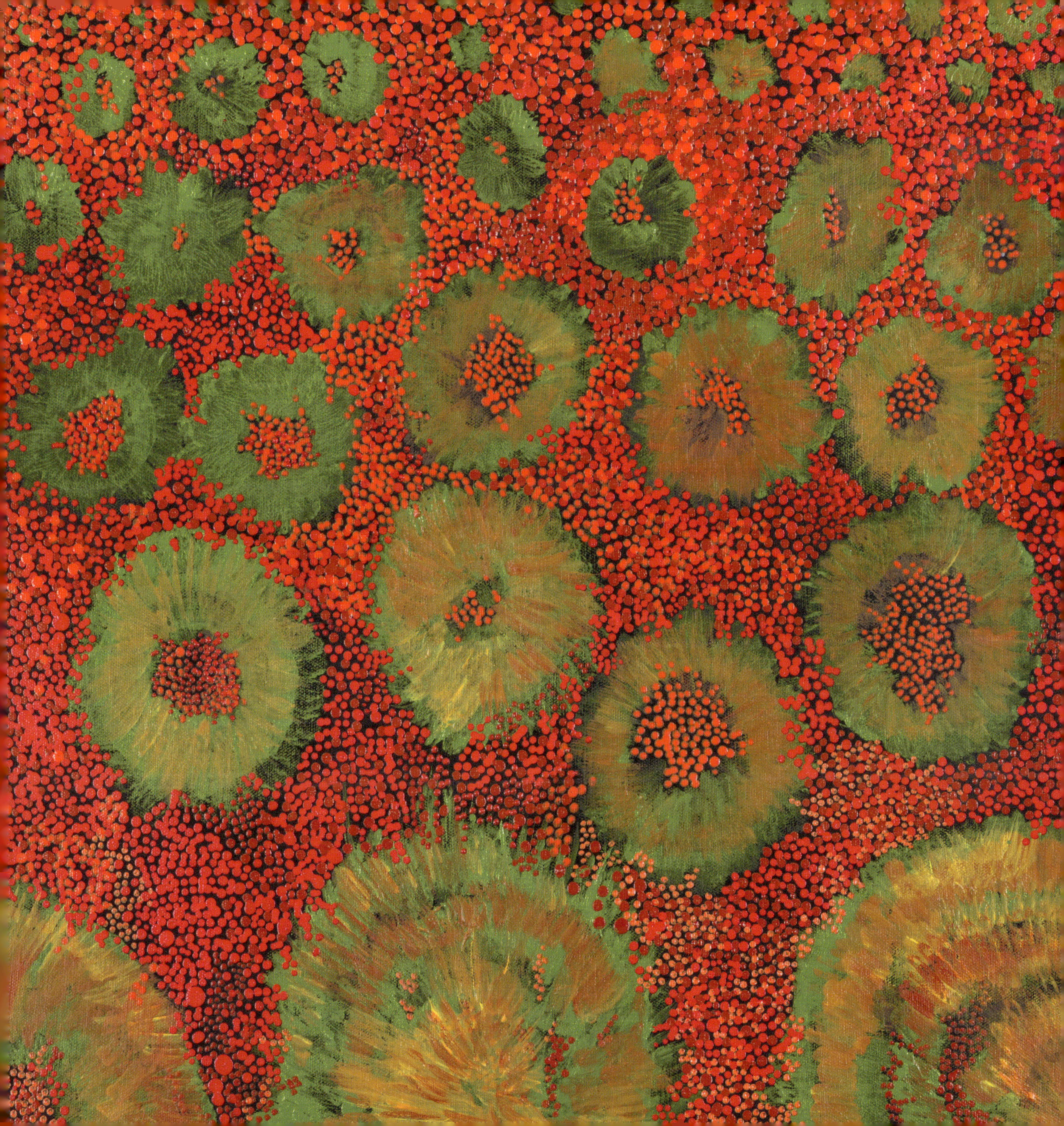

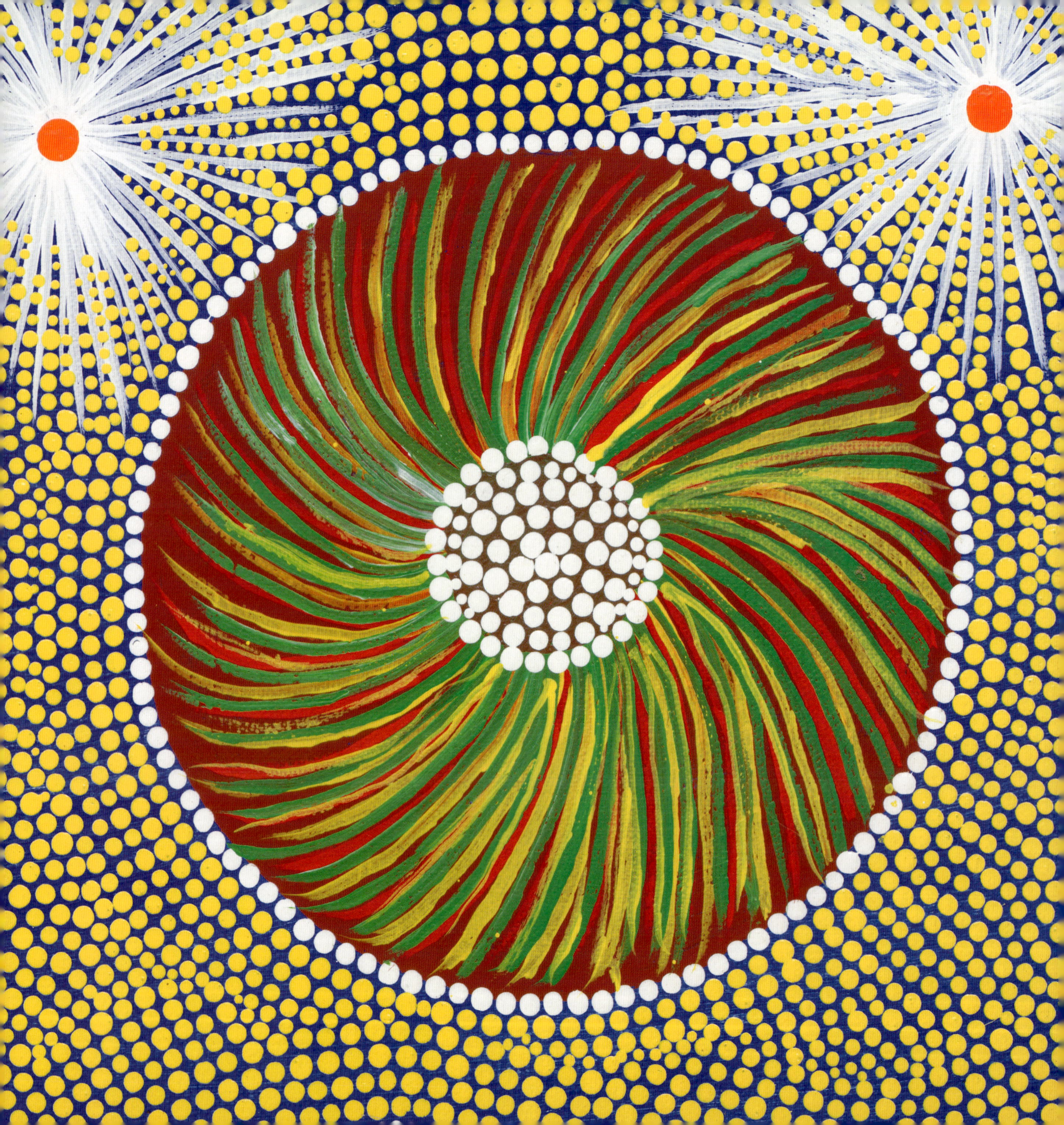

Warrwa-ngku im spredimat nyanuny pakamarraj wurrkal jalyi. Warrwa-ngku im gedimbat ngunti wulngarn-nginying. Im meikim sugar-ma grouimap-ku strongbala-wu.

The spinifex spread their spiky, green leaves. They capture light from the sun, to make the sugars they need to grow strong.

DID YOU KNOW?

Spinifex grass covers about one-third of Australia. It can handle lots of heat and live with very little water. Many kinds of spinifex can also recover quickly after fire. It's so tough that it can be used to strengthen car tyres, cement and sneakers!

Gurindji Kriol · English · Glossary word

Artist: Rachel Rennie

Wen dat warrwa im grouimap nyanuny olbala jalyi tarnim braunwan. Wen im makurru an jiwilying, nyilarrat munkurt-walija dei kamat an puntanup.

As the spinifex grows, their old leaves lose their colour. While the weather is humid, the termites can come to collect them.

DID YOU KNOW?

Many people think termites only eat wood, but this is not true. The termites in this book only eat spinifex grass (not your house!). In Gurindji language, termites are called munkurt.

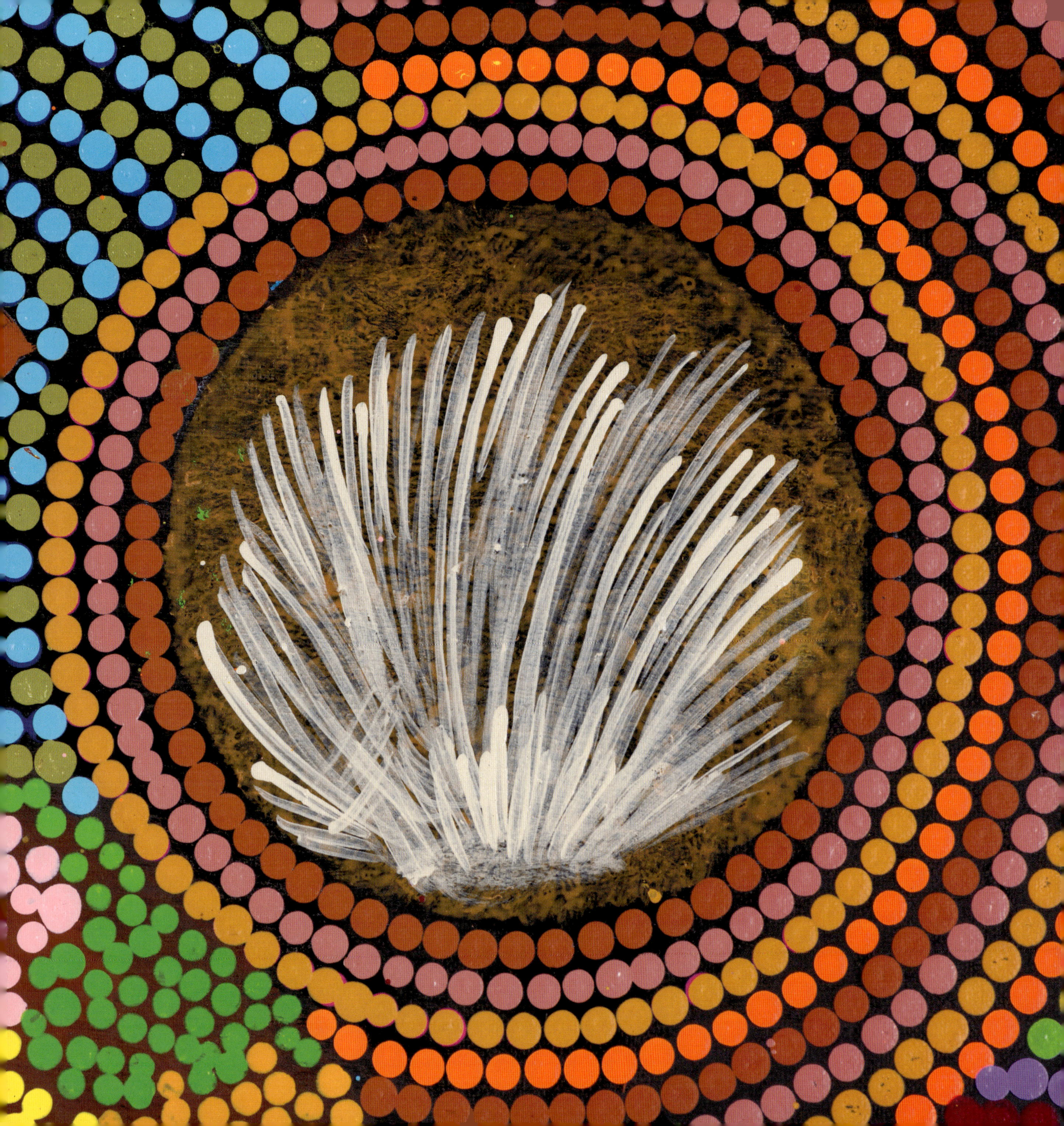

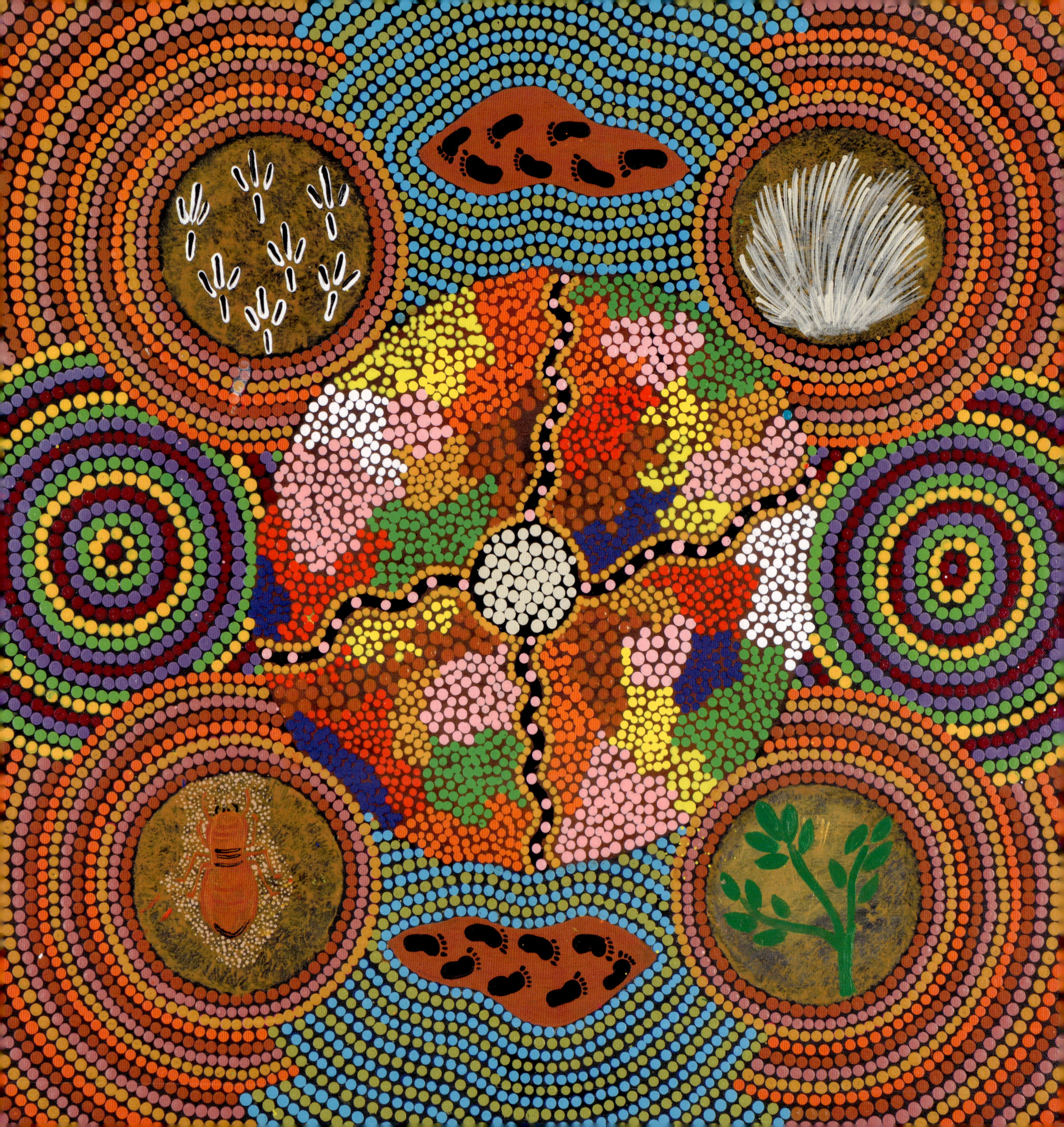

Dei gon walyak jimpiri-ngka, warukkaji munkurt-tu katimbat warrwa draiwan, and dei jarrpip teikimbek tamarra-ngkirri walyak.

Arriving through underground tunnels, each worker termite cuts pieces of dry spinifex, and carries them back to store in their mound.

DID YOU KNOW?

Most termites can't hear sound or see, but they get around by following vibrations and smells. They work together, without a leader, to complete different jobs for the good of the whole family. How's that for a deadly community!

Gurindji Kriol | English | Glossary word

Artist: Lucy Tanami

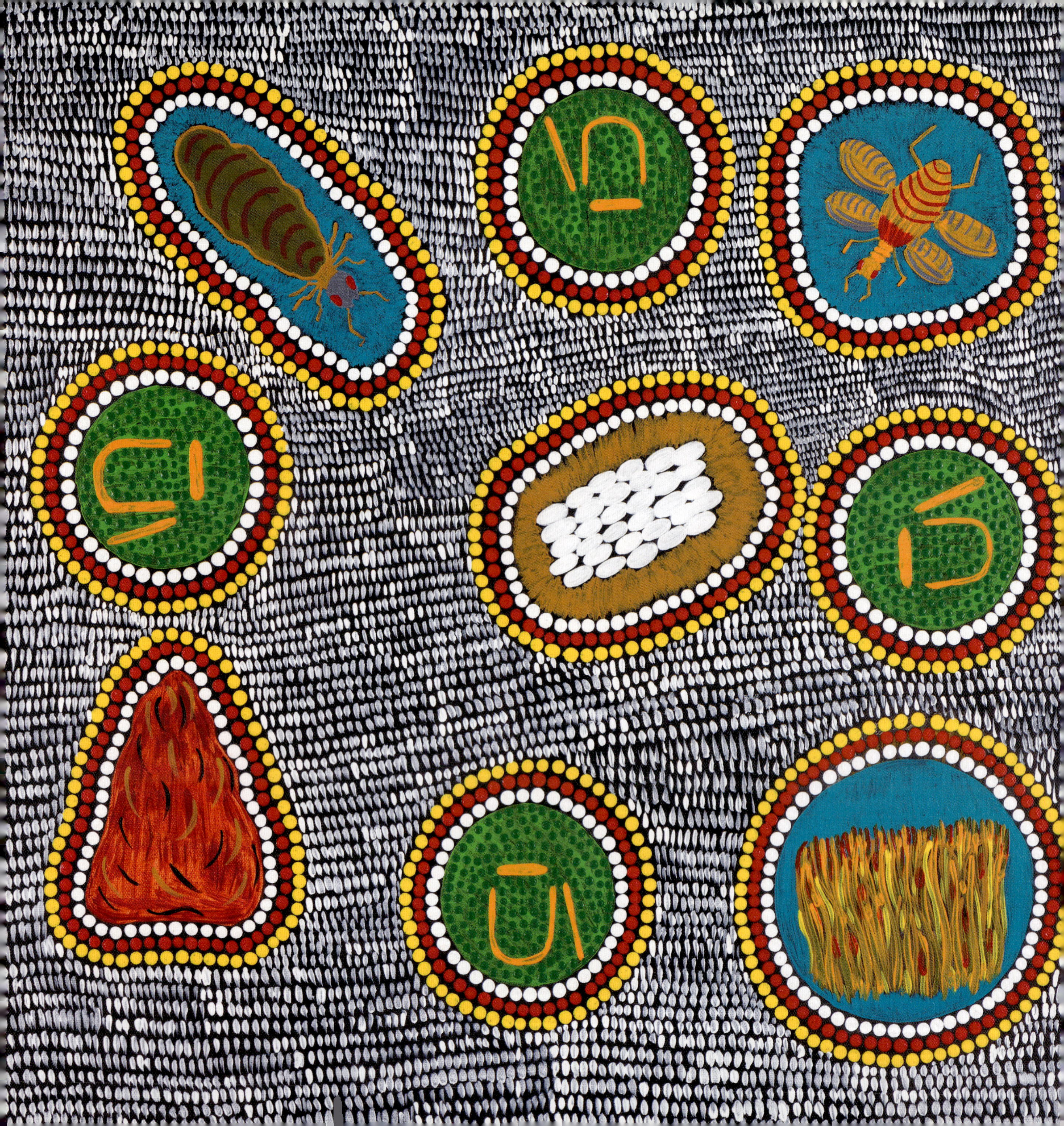

TAMARRA

TERMITE MOUND

Artist: Serena Donald

Tarlukurru-ngka walyak tamarra-ngka nyila munkurt-ku ngamayi meikimbat kampij. Warukkaji rarrarrajkarra tanku an klinimbatkarra nyanuny jangkarni puya. Jambala-ngku dei jarrpip nyanuny kampij yamak-tu juru-ngkirri.

Deep inside the mound, the termite mother is laying eggs. Workers rush about to feed and clean her enormous body. Some carry her eggs carefully to nearby nurseries.

DID YOU KNOW?

The mother termite lays a new egg every few seconds. That's 10,000 eggs a day and millions of eggs every year!

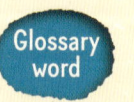

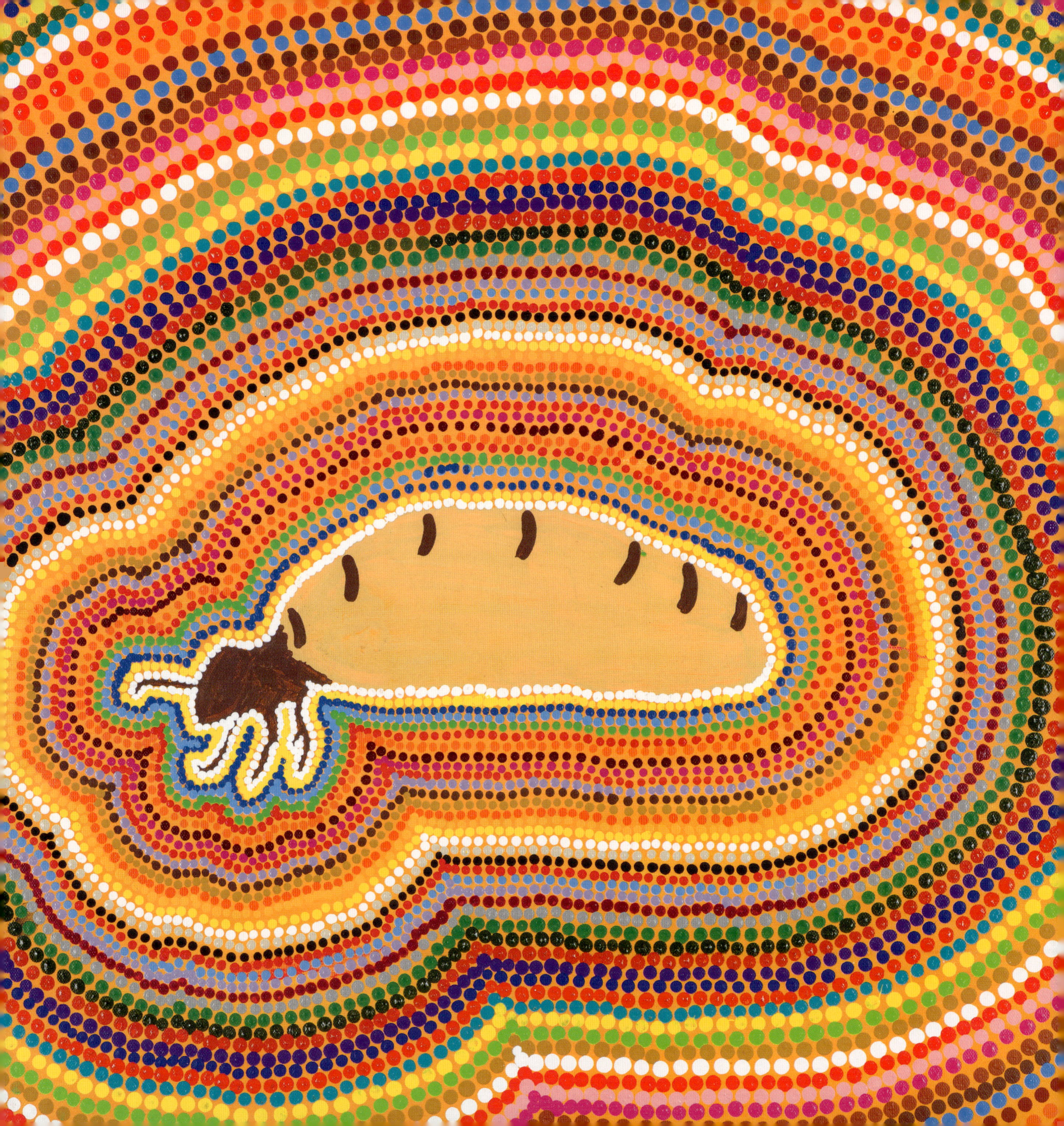

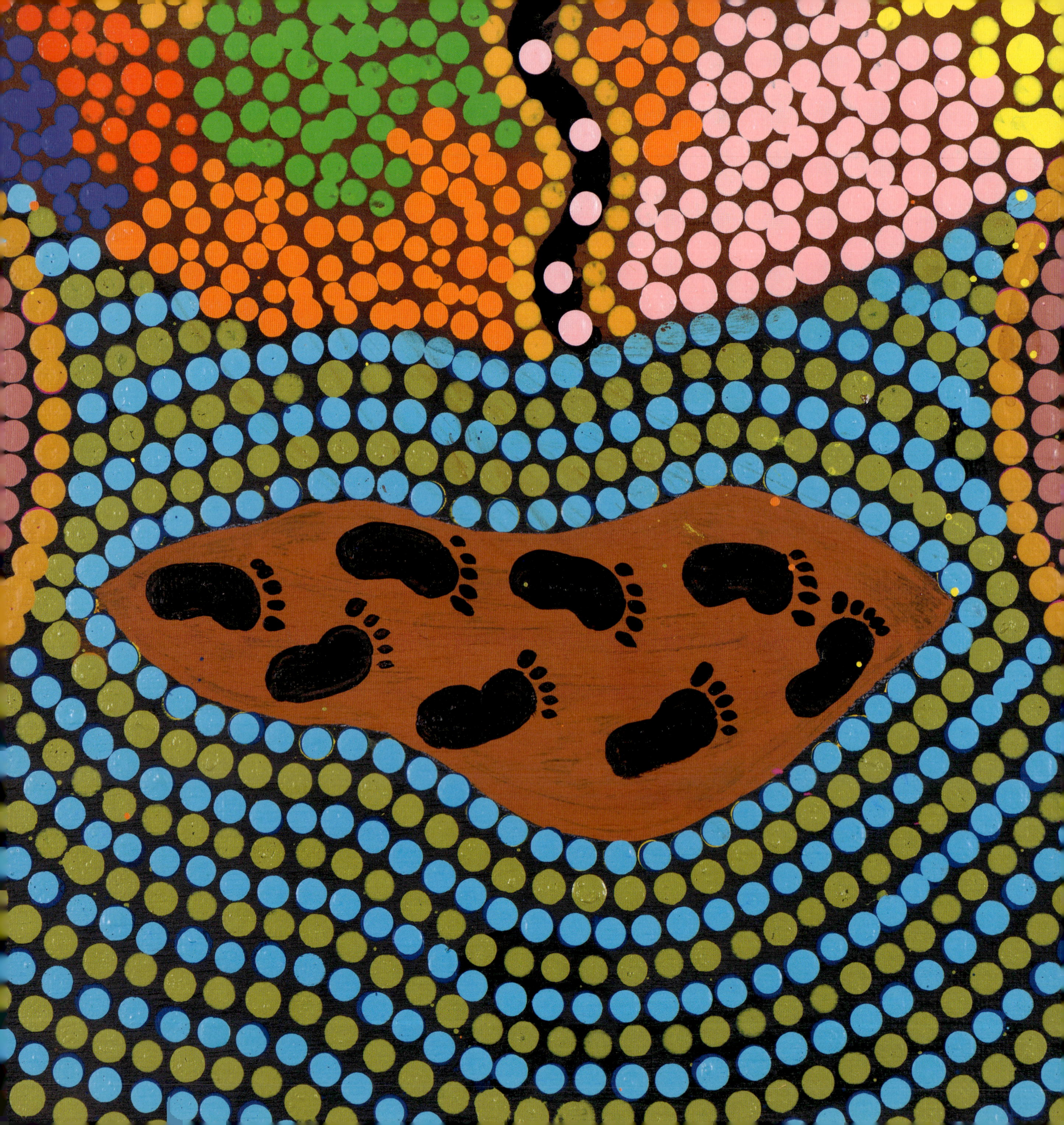

Tamarra-ma yingingingkarra signalku. Im meikim waringarri kilim nyarruluny ngarlaka kanyjurra floor-ngka. Kirri-walija jei kamap karnti-yawung meikim jimpiri nyila-ngka tamarra-ngka. Jei lakupkarra kampij-walija an putim kawarla-ngka jaartkarra-wu.

Defender termites beat their heads against the floor, creating an alarm signal that vibrates through the mound. Gurindji women have come with digging sticks to make a hole in the wall. They scoop out some eggs, sort them in a coolamon, and eat until they're full.

DID YOU KNOW?

Termites are often called 'white ants', but they are not related to ants at all. In fact, they evolved from wood-eating cockroaches about 155 million years ago during the time of the dinosaurs!

- Gurindji Kriol
- English
- Glossary word

Artist: Lucy Tanami

Dat warukkaji kurru dat signal-ma. Jei jikjikkarra jarrwalut purrpparni. Waringarri-walija walilikarra nyarruluny ngamayi to wajim dat jimpiri. Warukkaji jei waruk wajawaja pirrkap tamarra-wu wall-ma.

The worker termites respond to the alarm, arriving in huge numbers. While defenders form rings to protect their mother and guard the hole, workers quickly rebuild the wall.

DID YOU KNOW?

The hard outer wall of a termite mound is built from millions of tiny balls of soil that are stuck together with spit and 'poo glue'. The mound is like a fortress, helping to protect the termites from predators and fire.

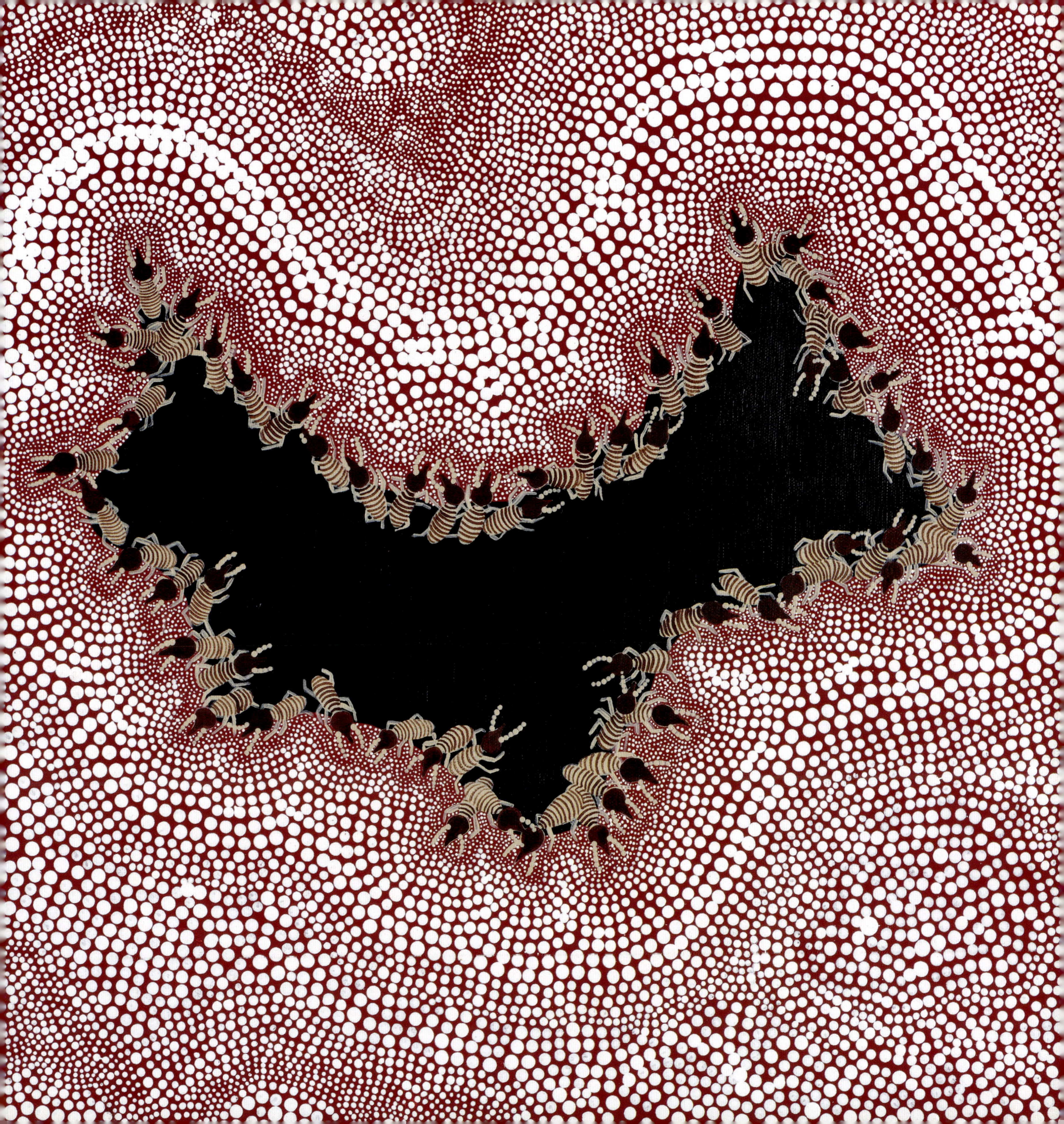

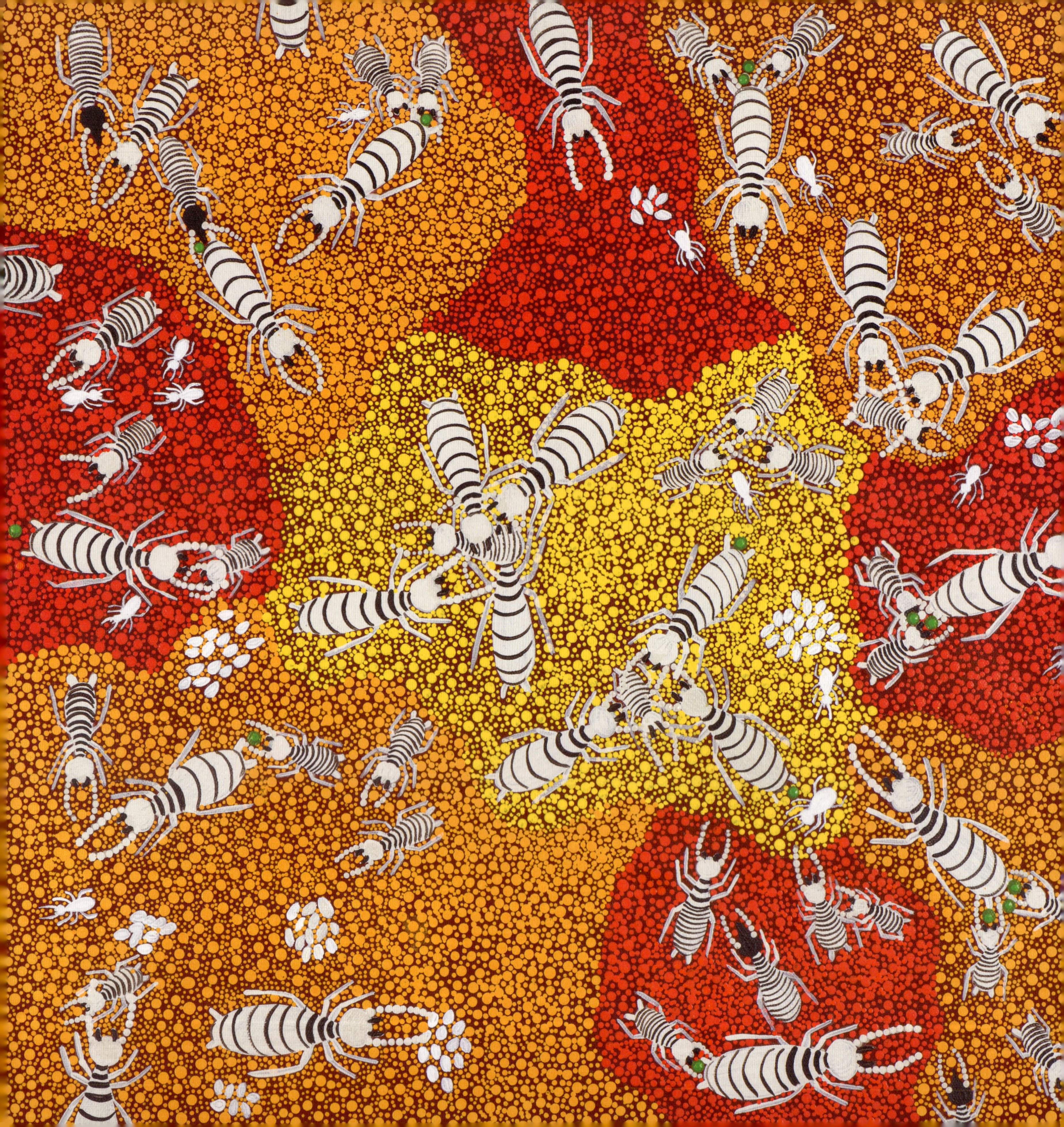

Nyila-nginying-ma pirrkap-nginying-ma tamarra-ma punyu na. Kapuku-ngku-ma jei fidimap nyanuny papa an kapuku strongbalak. Karu-nginying-ma jangkarni kapuku-ngku-ma jaartkarra nyarruluny yarrji.

After the damage is repaired, life in the mound returns to normal. Big sister termites feed their little brothers and sisters to make them strong. As the children grow, their family eat away their old layers of skin.

DID YOU KNOW?

Every termite begins their life in an egg. When they are born, they look like small, white versions of their parents. As they get bigger, they shed their skin. The worker termites eat these skins. How would you like a meal of skin?

Gurindji Kriol | English | Glossary word

Artists: Cecelia Edwards and Briony Barr

Kankulupal juru-ngka, jarrwalut karu-walija grouimap wings an mila. Jakiliny-kari-ngka-ma redibala tiwu na.

In special chambers above the nurseries, one group of children are growing wings and eyes.
In a few months, they will be ready to fly.

DID YOU KNOW?

Each termite family begins with a new mother and father (sometimes called the queen and king). The father always stays with the mother, and mother termites are one of the longest living insects in the world. Some live up to 25 years!

Gurindji Kriol · English · Glossary word

Artists: Briony Barr, Caroline Jimmy and Cecelia Edwards

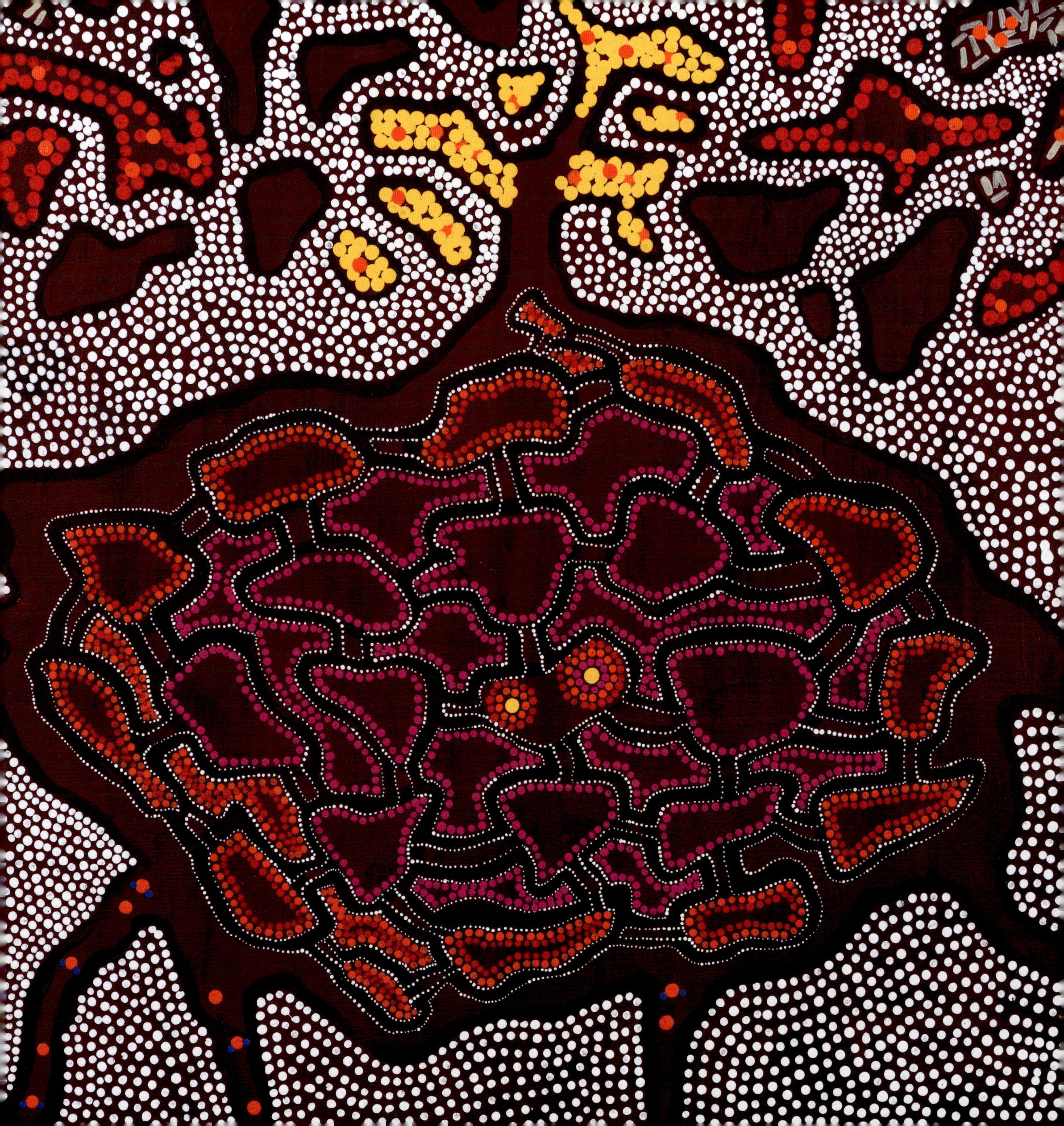

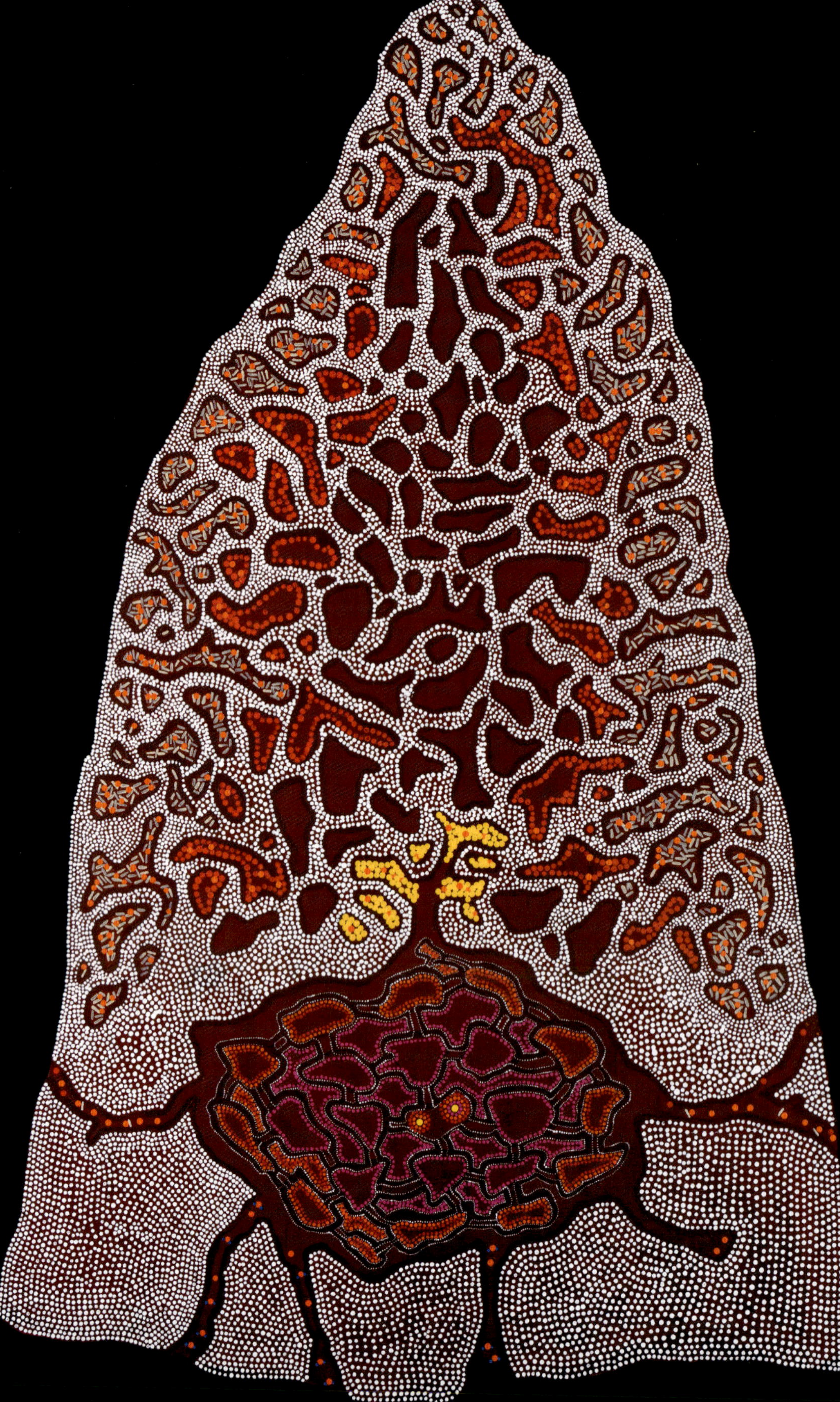

Kankula partaj-ja nyilarrat waringarri-ma karrap-ku, redibala sprayimbat-ku poison nyarruluny ngarlaka-nginying. Dei wajim nyarruluny ngurra jungkuwurru-nginying an pingi-walija-nginying.

Higher up the mound, the defender termites are always on guard, ready to spray sticky poison from their heads to defend their home against invading echidnas or armies of ants.

DID YOU KNOW?

Defender termites (also known as soldiers) have a pointed head, which is like a glue gun – it can spray strands of sticky liquid which ties the ants' legs up in knots! It also tastes disgusting, so bigger predators like lizards and echidnas back off. Never mess with a defender termite!

Gurindji Kriol · English · Glossary word

Artists: Briony Barr, Caroline Jimmy and Cecelia Edwards

Kanyjupal tamarra-ngka
warukkaji-ngku
karankarra kanyjurrak
ngawa-wu.
Jei kambek garram clay
to pirrkap dat tamarra
strongbalak,
ngawa dei sharim
gat nyarruluny femli.

Under the mound, workers
dig deep tunnels down to
the water table below.
They return with mineral-rich
clay for building the
mound up strong,
and water to share
with their thirsty family.

DID YOU KNOW?

During the dry season, worker termites build and travel through tunnels down to water deep in the ground, sometimes as deep as 80 metres. That's almost the same height as the Statue of Liberty in the USA or London's Big Ben!

Gurindji Kriol | English | Glossary word

Artist: Violet Wadrill

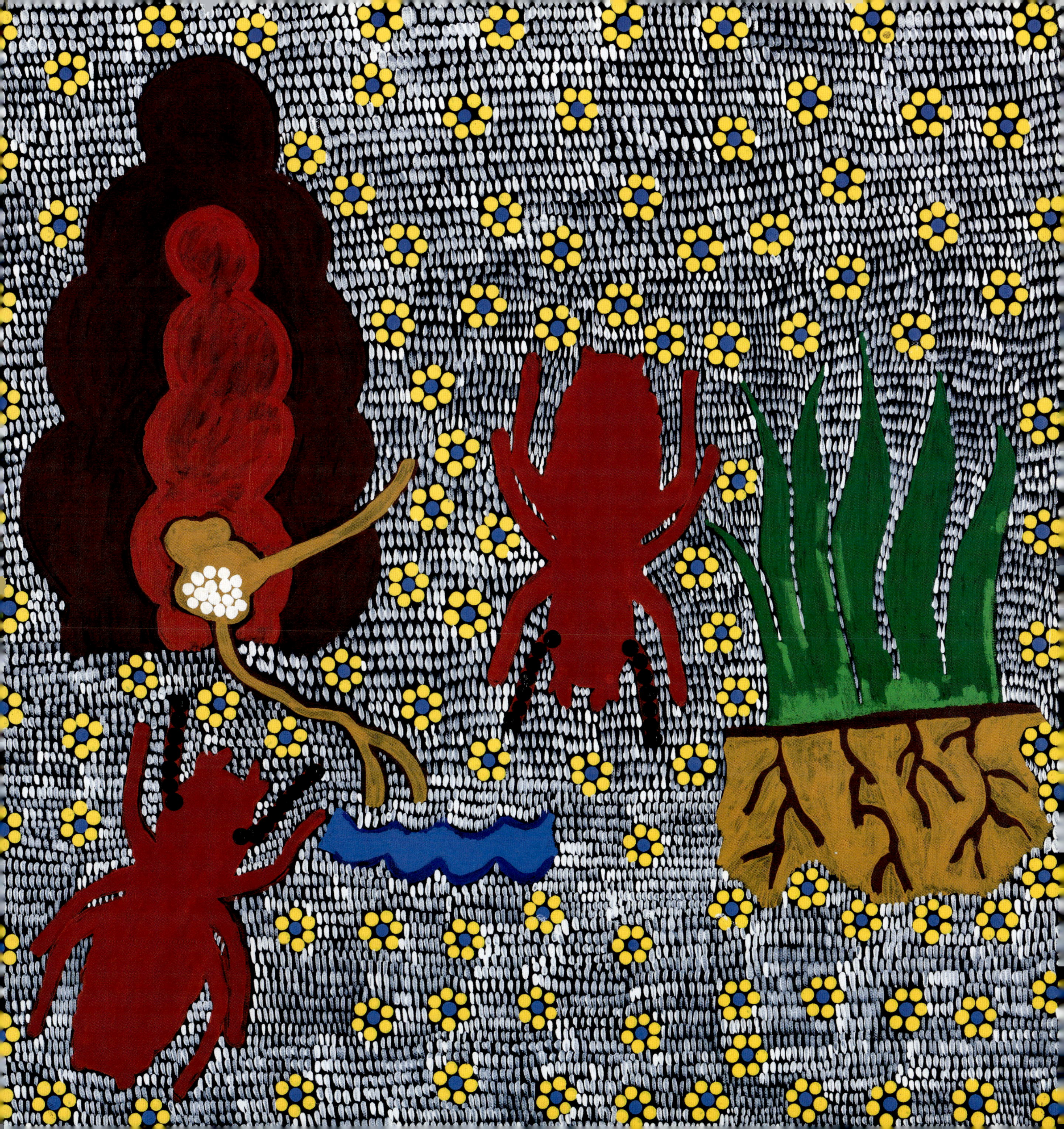

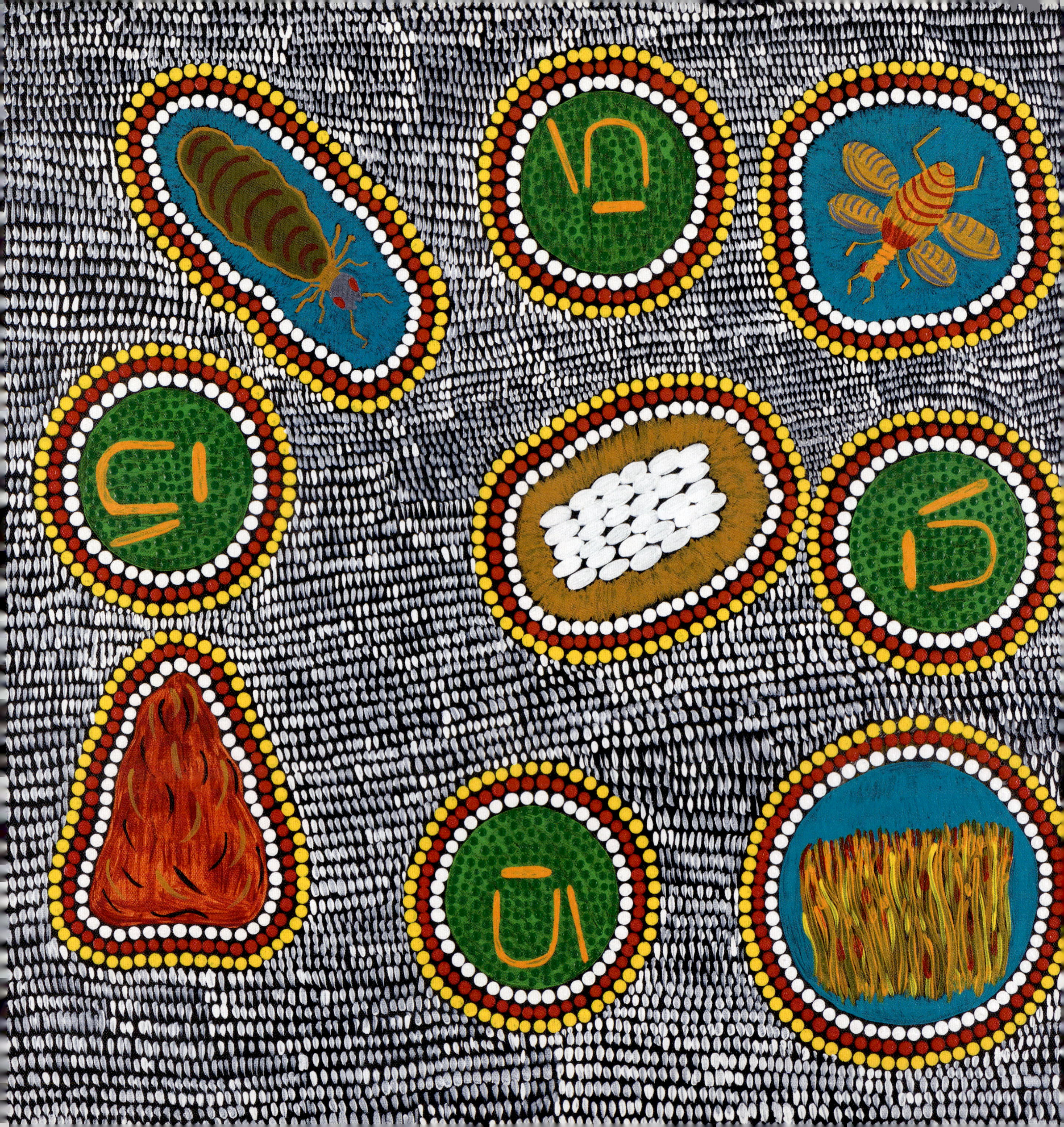

MAJUL

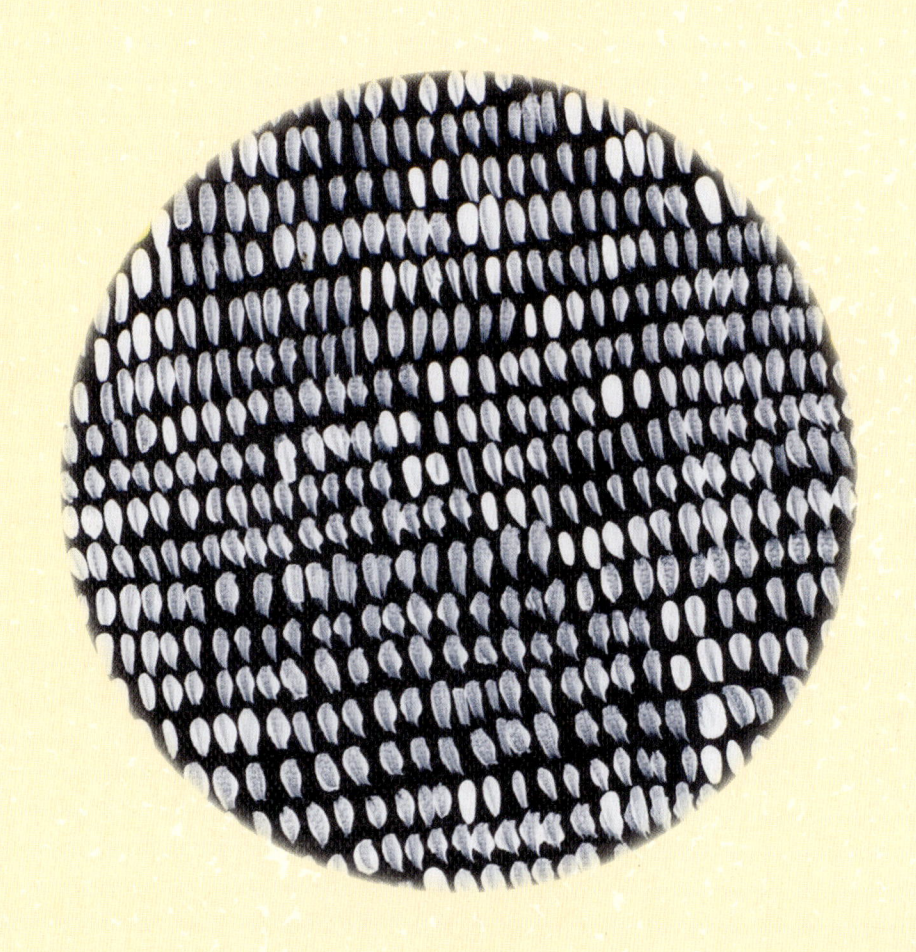

GUT

Artist: Serena Donald

Warukkaji-ngku im habim ngilyjik warrwa-ma yapayapa. Yapakayi fibre im gon puya-ngkirri walyak, yalanginying-ma im gon majul-ta walyak weya im liwart bacteria …

A **worker** termite chews and swallows a piece of spinifex grass. Tiny fibres travel through their body, and finally arrive in the gut, where the bacteria are waiting …

DID YOU KNOW?

Termites are one of the few animals that can eat the tough, dry leaves of the spinifex plant. How would you feel about spinifex for dinner?

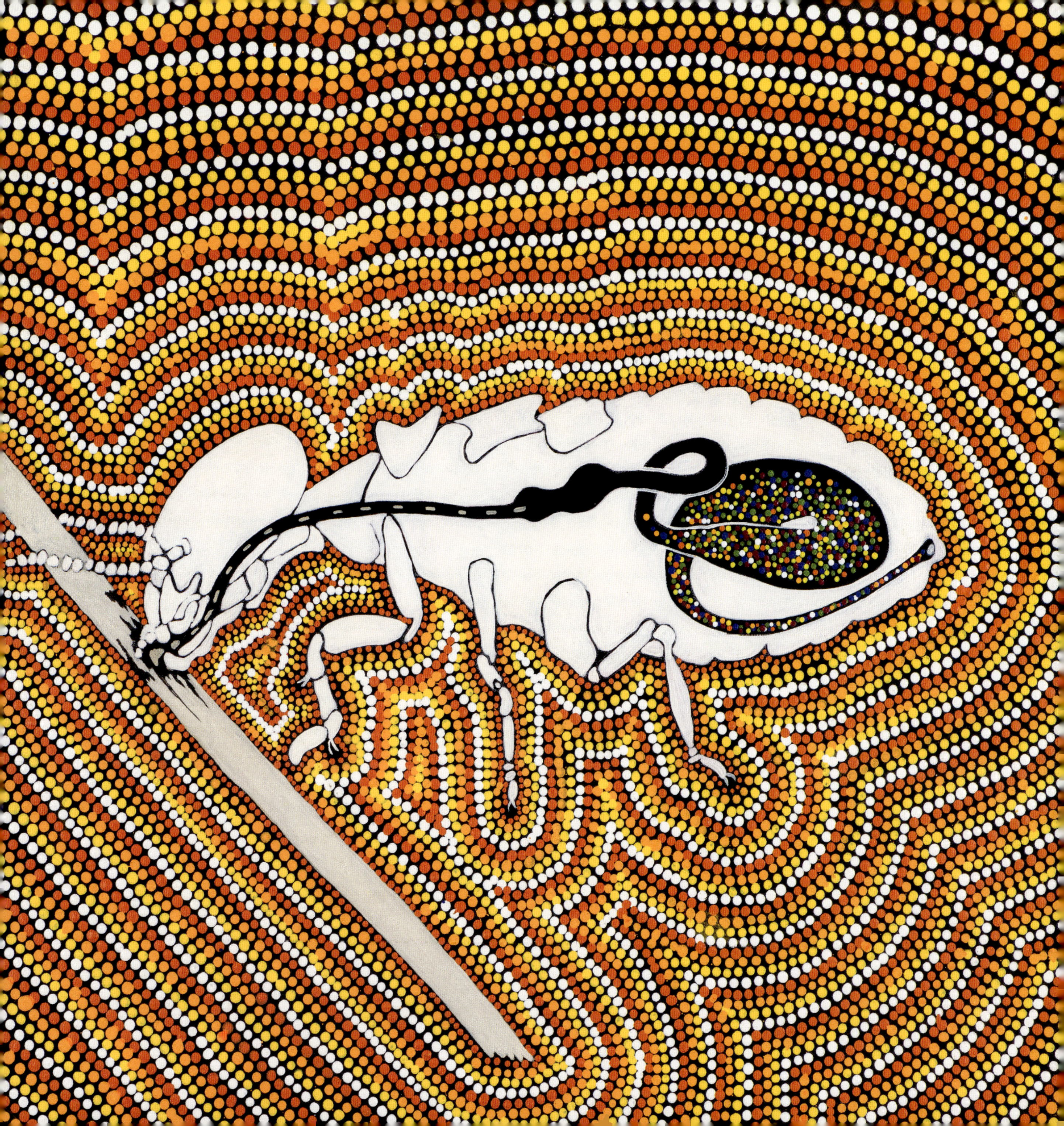

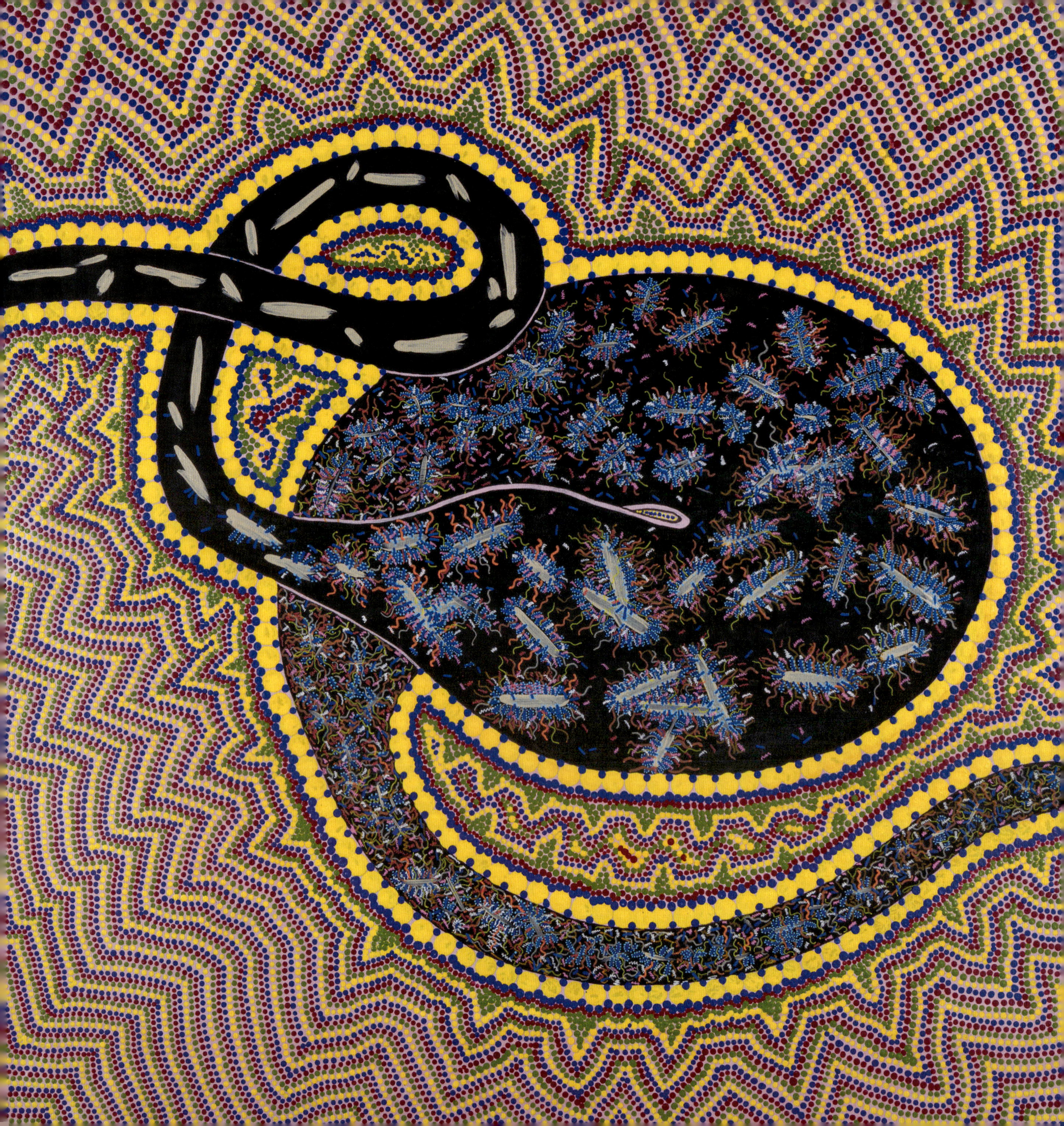

Jarrwalut bacteria kirt warrwa fibre an gedim sugar walyak. Najalot meikim dat sugar into energy, an jambala-ngku meikim protein munkurt-ku.

Millions of bacteria break the spinifex fibres apart, to get to the sugars inside. Other bacteria transform the sugars into energy, and some make protein for the termite.

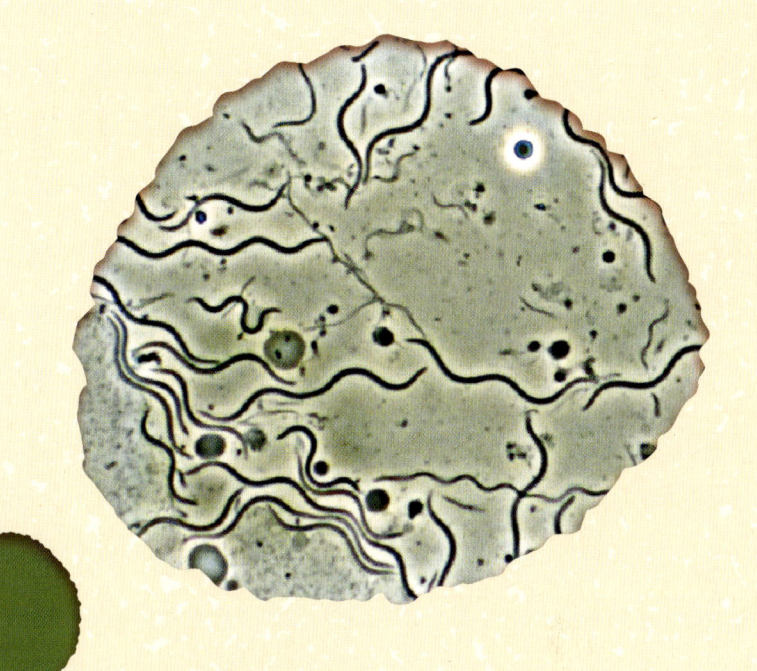

DID YOU KNOW?

All animals (including you) have tiny creatures in their gut called bacteria (see image above). Termites couldn't live without these friends who turn spinifex grass into food and energy. Go team!

Gurindji Kriol · English · Glossary word

Artists: Briony Barr, Joanne Stevens, Margaret Winbye, Gregory Crocetti and Year 2/3/4 Kalkaringi School students

55

Warukkaji sharimbat tanku majul-nginying, punyu tanku walyak ngamayi-yu an nyanuny karu-wu, an jamtaim nangkaji pirrkap-ku tamarra-wu strongbala-wu.

The worker termite can now share food from their gut, a nutritious poo, a meal fit for a queen and her children, and sometimes a glue for building strong walls.

DID YOU KNOW?

Termites just love poo! They create four different kinds (see p. 5). In fact, they love it so much that they eat it *and* build houses with it. All day long they're having a 'pooping' good time!

Gurindji Kriol · English · Glossary word

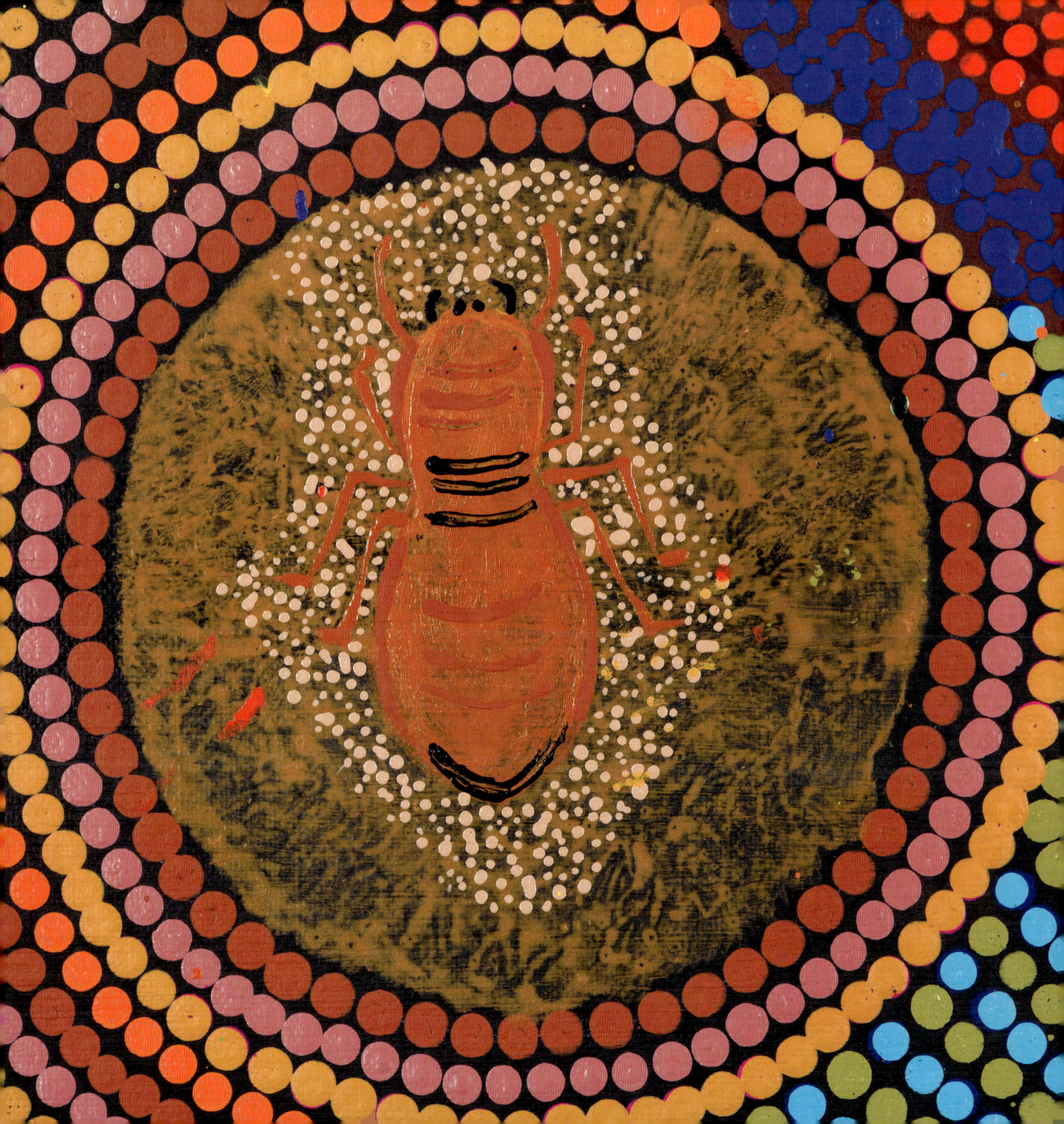

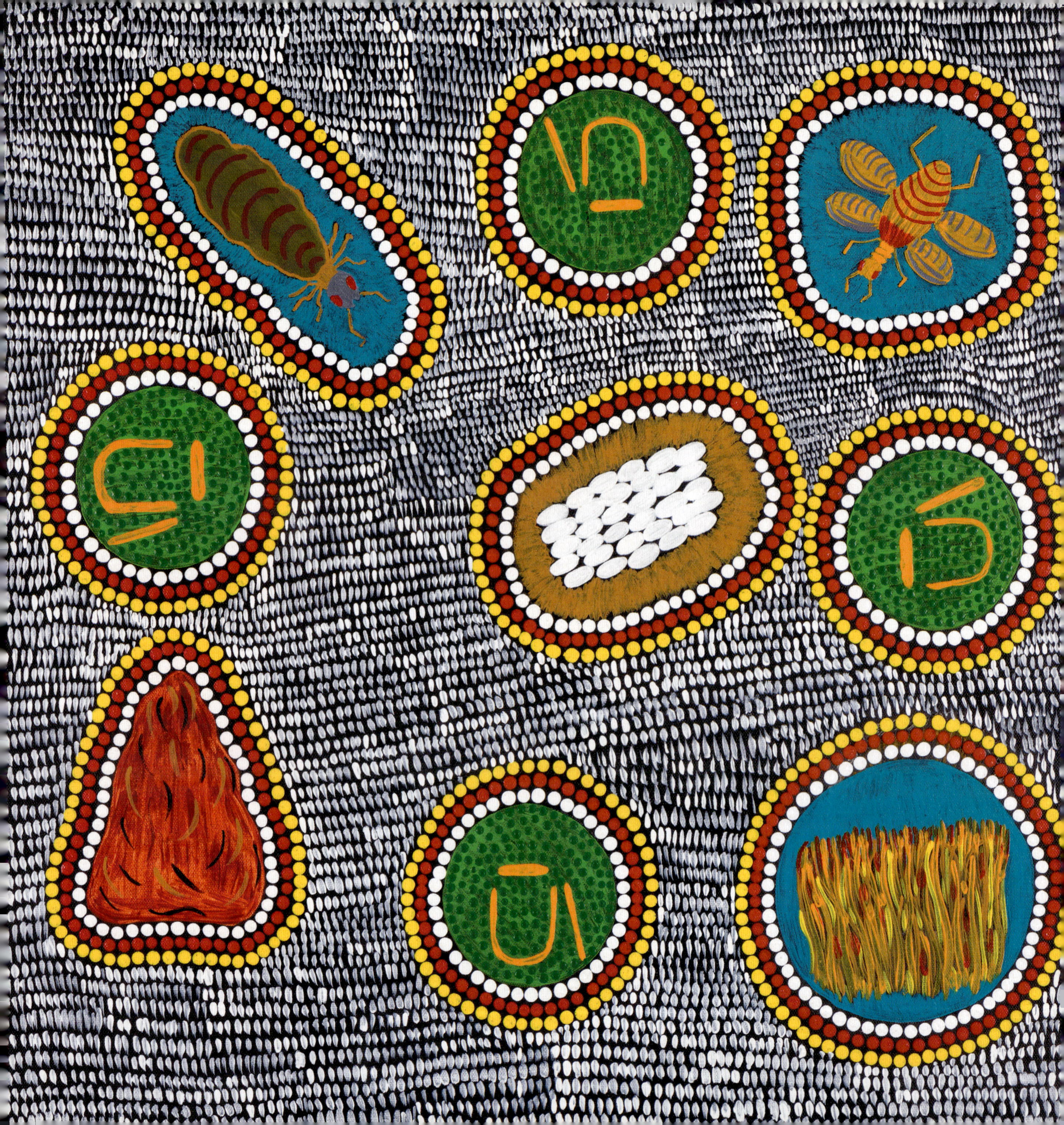

YIPUNGKA

RAINTIME

Artist: Serena Donald

Abta-ma ngajik-nginying, draiwan-nginying-ma ngawa na im baldan. Ngawa-ma parrngany janyja-ngka-ma an jakarr munkurt-ku jimpiri. Warukkaji-ngku im gedim ngawa yapakayi to meikim dat tamarra.

After the long dry, the rains return. Water soaks into the ground through termite tunnels. The worker termites collect the droplets to help build the mound.

DID YOU KNOW?

There are three main seasons on Gurindji Country – the wet season, the dry season and the build-up season where it gets hotter and wetter over a few months. It can get up to 45 degrees Celcius!

Gurindji Kriol • English • Glossary word

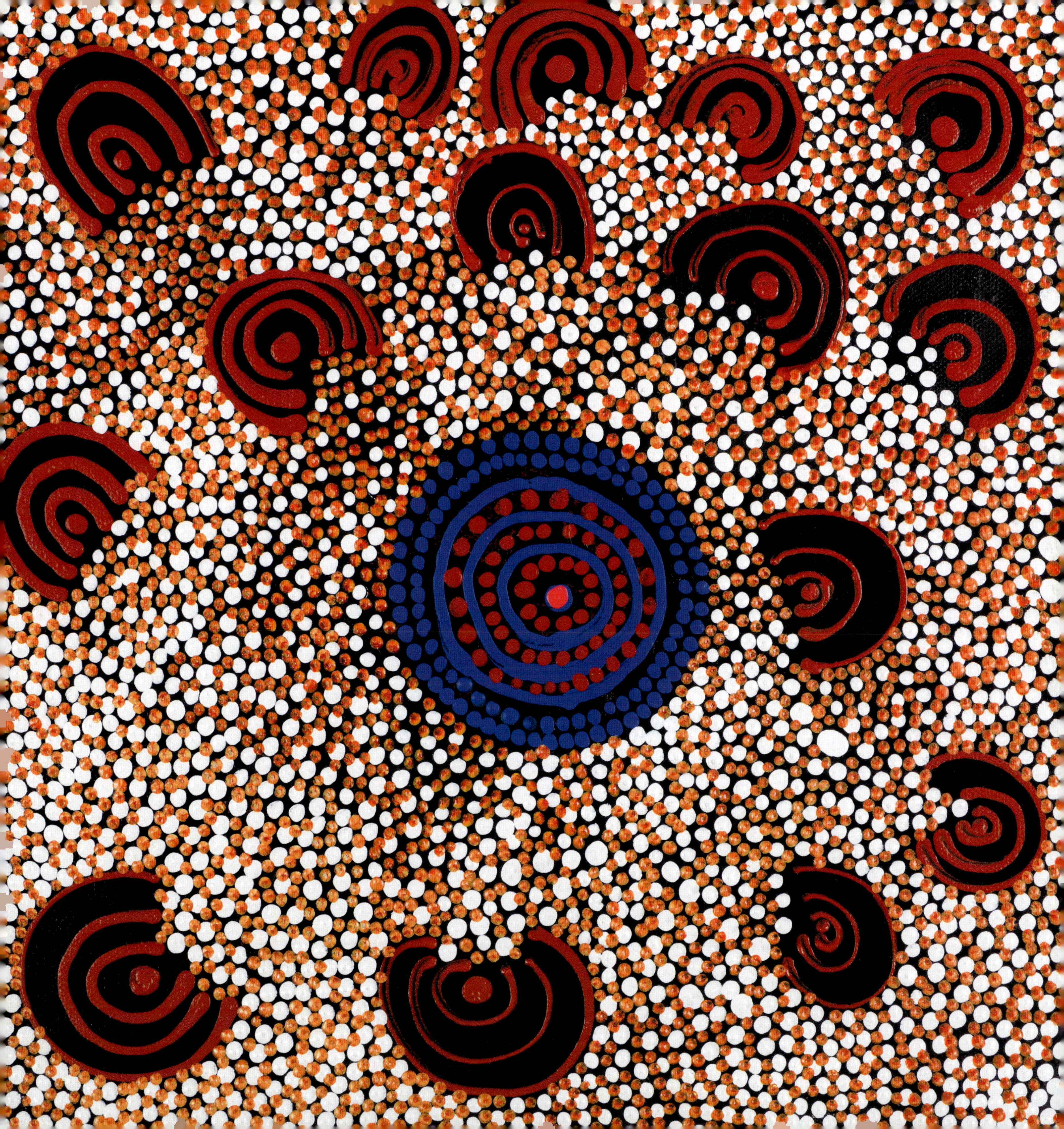

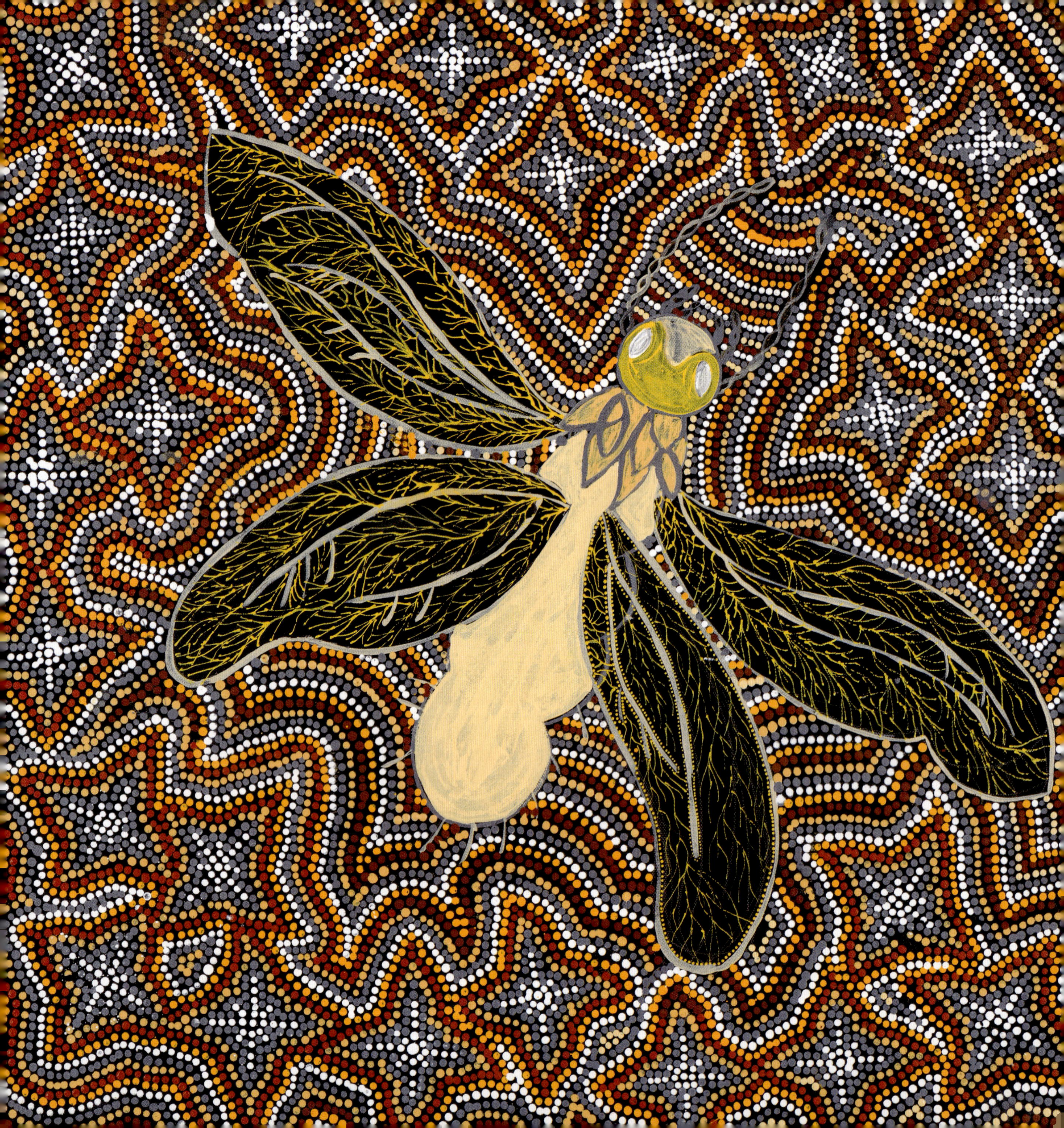

Abta rein dat janyja
im kalypa,
an sign bo pirna
to libim tamarra.
Dei partaj kankulak
an tiwu kaputa-ngka.

After good rain,
the ground becomes soft,
a sign for the
winged termites
to leave the mound.
They climb to the top
and launch into the night.

DID YOU KNOW?

About once a year, the mother termite produces a special batch of eggs. These become winged termites that will be future mothers and fathers of new termite families.

Gurindji Kriol | English | Glossary word

Artist: Cecelia Edwards and Briony Barr

Likarta, pingi, jiika, jurlaka dei ngarramkap dat tiwuwaji, an dei juwarrp tanku-yu. Tamarra-nginying-kari tamarra-nginying-kari tiwuwaji jikkarra.

The swarms of flying termites attract lizards, ants, bilbies and birds, who gather for the feast. Mound after mound, erupts with food.

DID YOU KNOW?

Lots of animals love to eat termites. Likarta (lizards), tarru (spiders), jurlaka (birds), ngakparn (frogs), wari (snakes) and jiika (bilbies) all hunt them down because they are so tasty.

Gurindji Kriol | English | Glossary word

Artist: Sophia Donnelly-Patterson

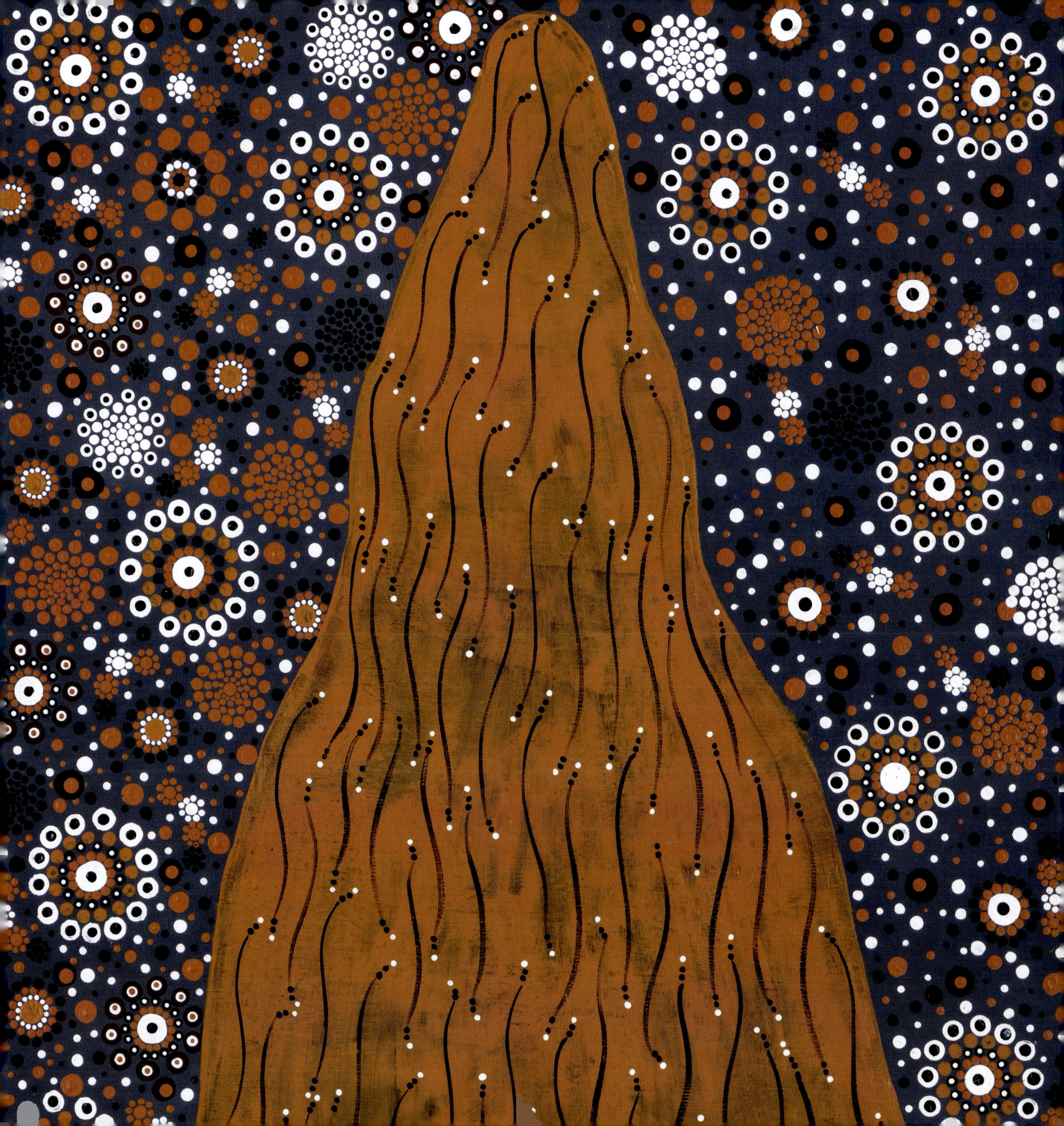

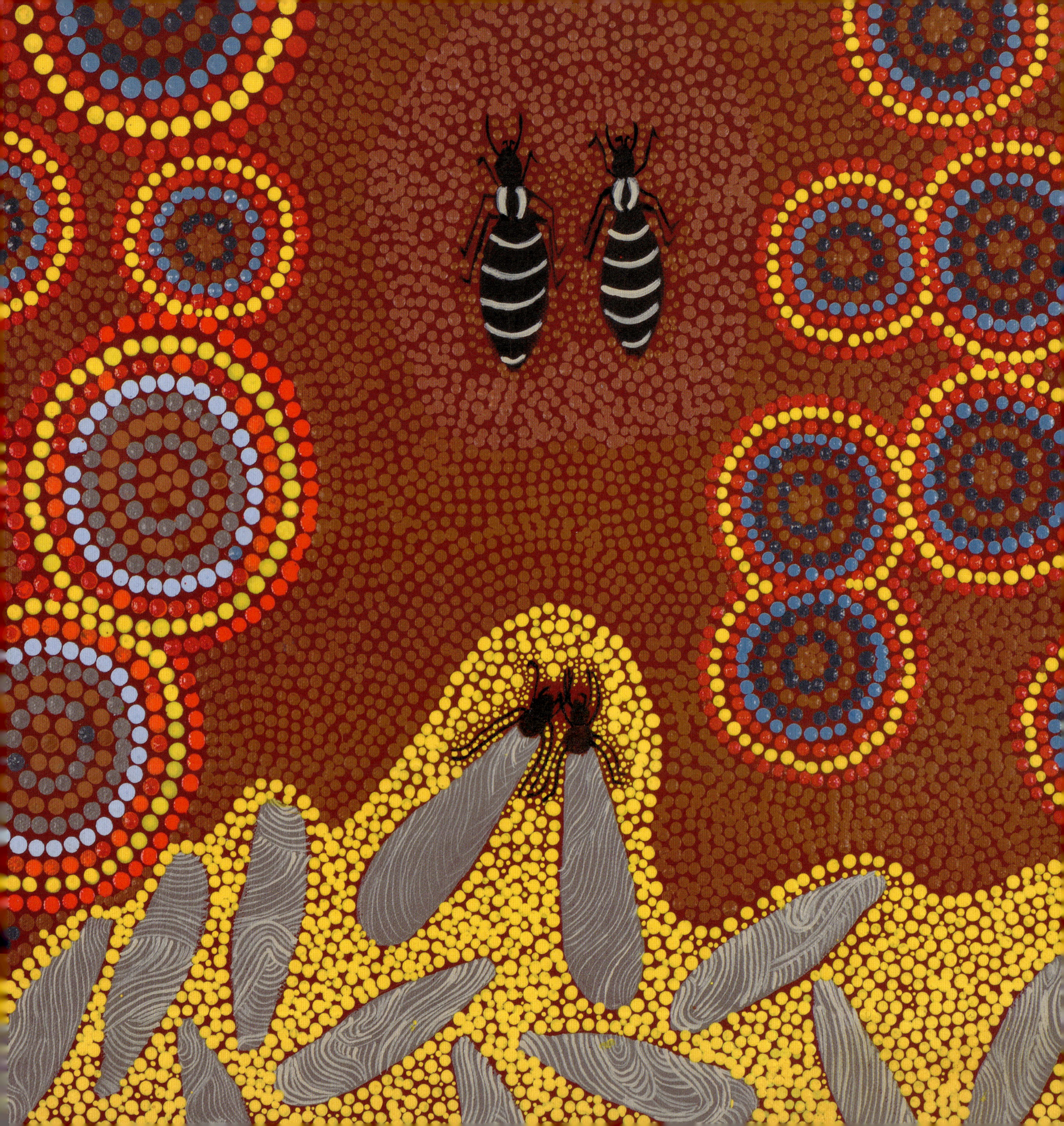

Tiwuwaji-kujarra tilwak an dei faindim mijelp. Kanyjupal dei libim nyarruluny wing ngumayila an jarrartpurru. Jei karankarra sofwan janyja-ngka.

Two winged termites escape the hungry mouths and find each other. Leaving their wings behind, they run together. And on a soft patch of soil, they start to dig.

DID YOU KNOW?

When a young female termite lands, she sprays a chemical into the air that attracts male termites. To them it smells like the most wonderful perfume! What is your favourite smell?

Ngamayi-ma karu-yawung na. Ib jei wanji dat tamarra im til kutij ngajik, im nurt Kantri an stat igin.

A new family begins with these young mother and father termites. If the family survives, their mound will last many generations, before returning to Country.

DID YOU KNOW?

Termite mounds can be up to 8 metres high, making them the tallest structures in the animal world. They are natural skyscrapers!

Gurindji Kriol · English · Glossary word

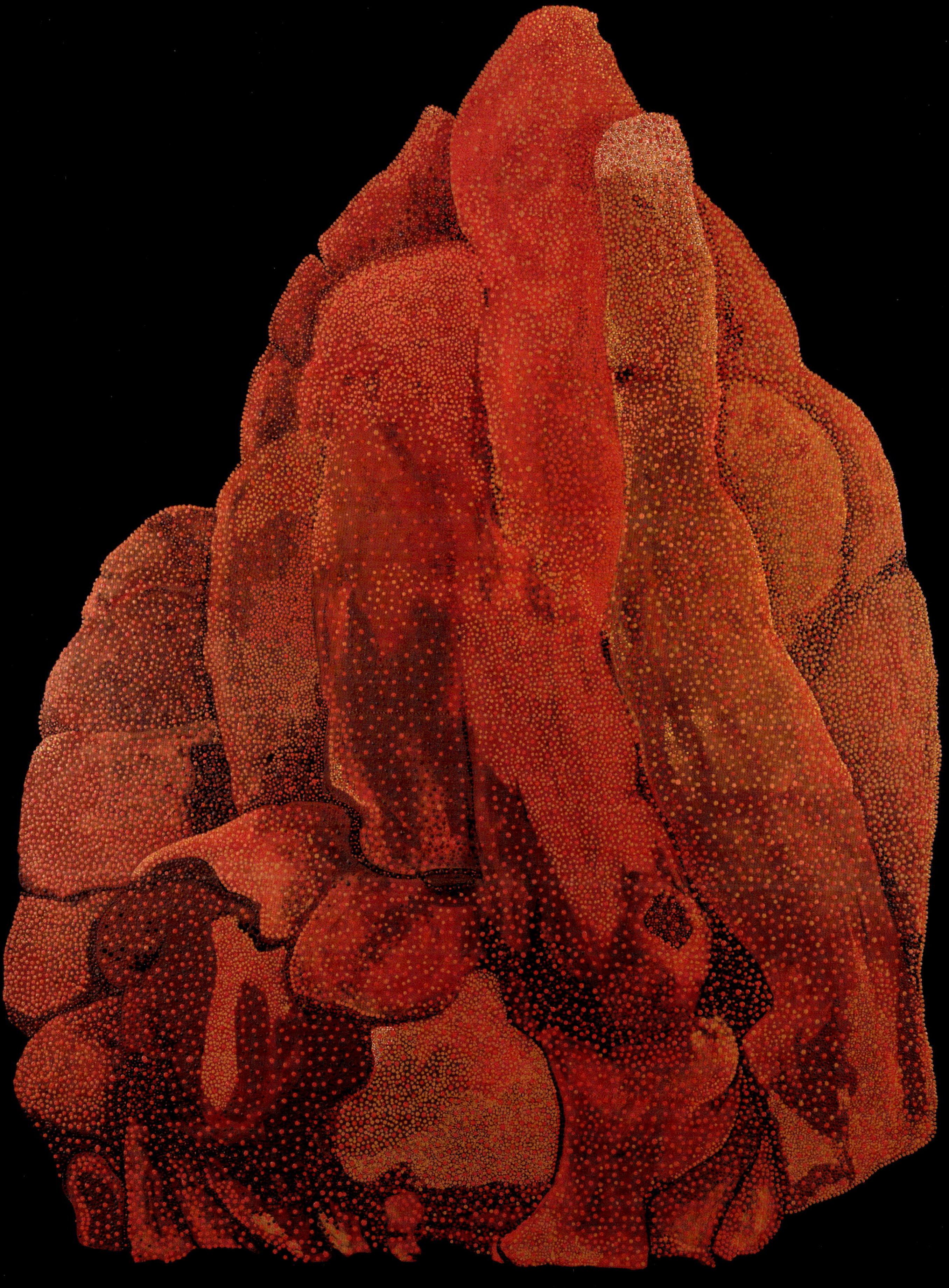

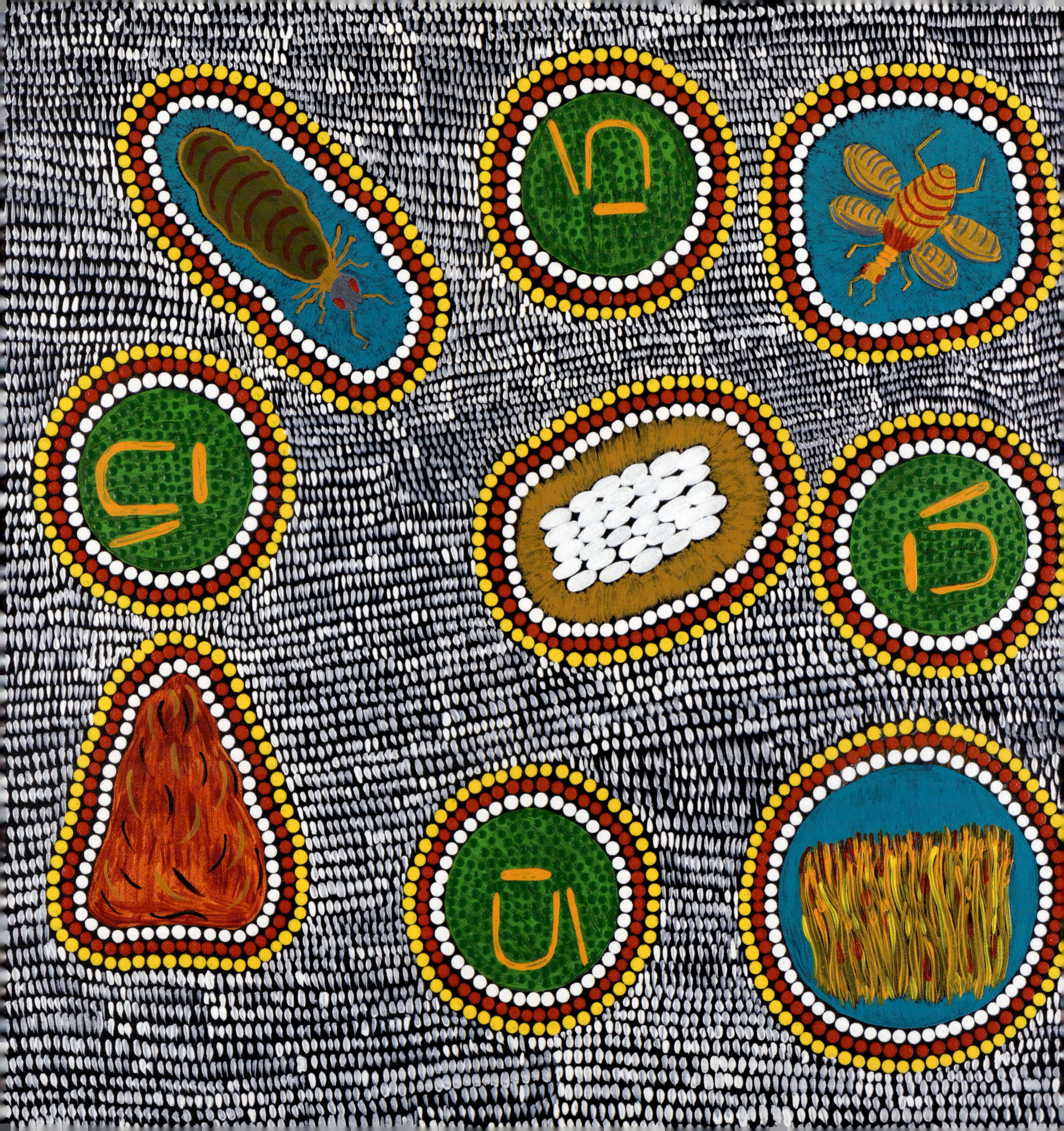

NGUMAYIJANG

FUTURE GENERATIONS

Artist: Serena Donald

**Jangkarni karru-nga.
Karru-nga nyanuny
kaminyjarr.
Nyantu na kamparnana
karu-ma ngunyunu
kamparnana.
Yumi ngulu
ngarrka manku.**

The baby has grown up and now has grandchildren of their own. The grandmother will treat them with termite mound and keep Gurindji culture strong.

DID YOU KNOW?

First Nations People have lived on this continent for thousands of generations. They are the oldest continuous living culture in the world. Now, that's the deadliest fact of all!

Gurindji | English | Glossary word

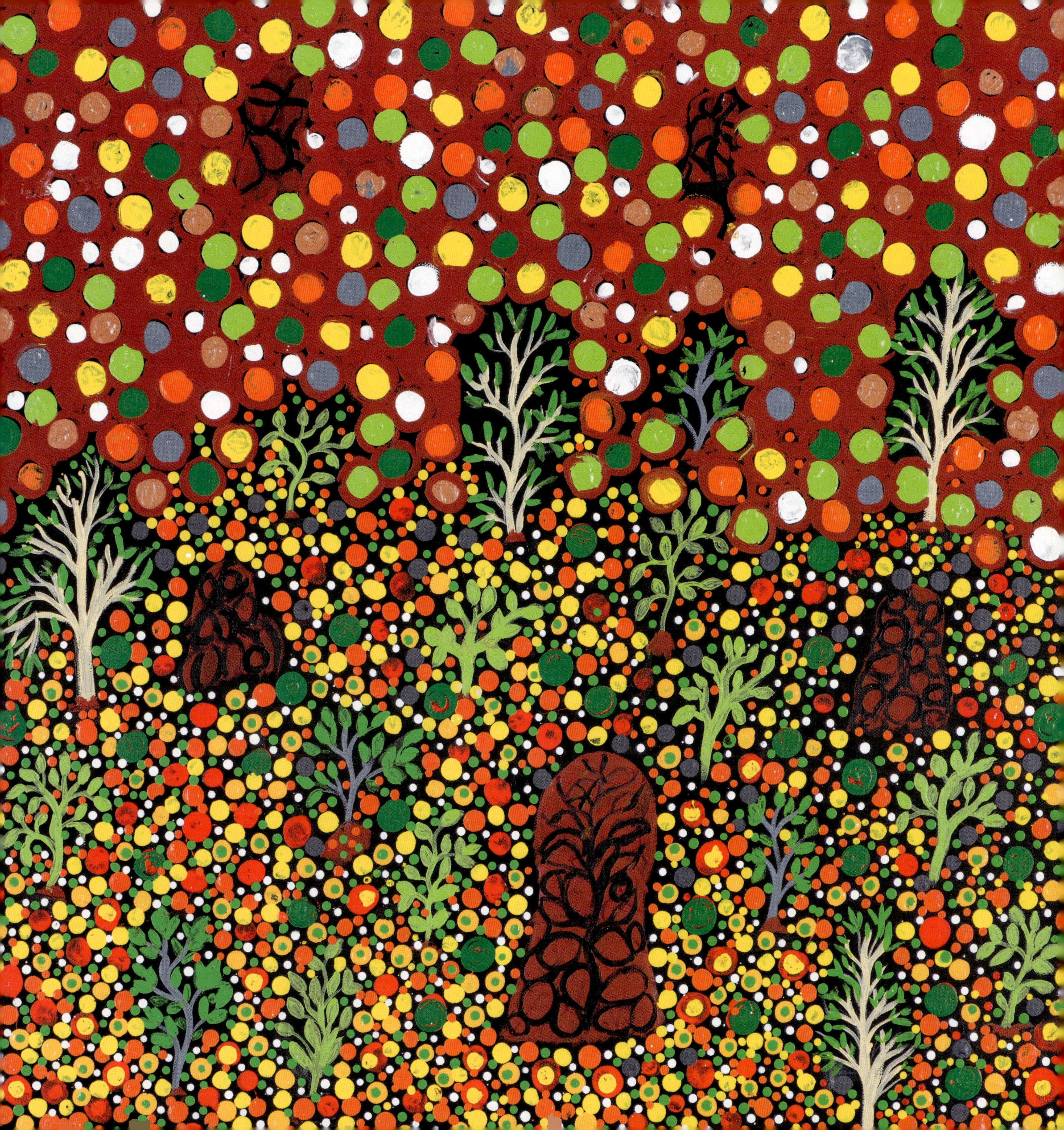

BEHIND THE STORY

Gurindji Country

Gurindji history begins with the creation of the land during the Puwarraj (Dreaming). The hills, rocks, rivers, waterholes and trees were made, along with animals, humans, rain and lightning.

Caring for Country is important to Gurindji People. For thousands of years before European invasion, Gurindji People lived close to major rivers where they speared fish, or caught them in fish traps called puul. Gurindji People also used fire to herd kangaroos and wallabies, and caught large birds using traps called larrkan. Fire was also used to help plants grow.

Gurindji People grew large janangarn (gardens) of bush cucumbers and yams. They also ate fruit, other root vegetables and grains, and created bush medicines using local plants and animals (including termite mound).

The arrival of kartiya

Kartiya (non-Indigenous people) first came to Gurindji Country in the 1860s. This was a terrible time for the Gurindji People. Farmers took over Gurindji Country to set up big cattle stations. The cattle destroyed the janangarn and langkarna (waterholes) and it became more and more difficult for Gurindji People to look after Country.

View from Mt Possum on Gurindji Country

Bush bananas (kilipi)

Kartiya forced Gurindji people to work on the cattle stations. Gurindji workers and their families were not paid or given enough food to eat. From 1910, children with a Gurindji mother and kartiya father were taken away from their mothers and sent to grow up far from their families. These people are now a part of Australia's Stolen Generations.

The Wave Hill Walk-off

In 1966, about 200 Gurindji and other First Nations men and women stopped working and walked off Wave Hill Station. They wanted to stand up to the kartiya and make them understand that the workers should not be treated this way.

In 1975, Gough Whitlam, who was prime minister at the time, decided to give back a small bit of land to Gurindji People. In 1986, this decision was made official. Then, in 2020, Gurindji People were given Native Title rights over Wave Hill Station. This means that the government agreed that the Gurindji People have a deep connection to their land and always will.

Gurindji strikers in the dry river bed of the Victoria River, 1966

Freedom Day, 23 August 2016, the 50th anniversary of the Wave Hill Walk-Off

Gurindji, Gurindji Kriol and Kriol languages

Today, Gurindji Elders speak traditional Gurindji and younger generations speak Gurindji Kriol.

Gurindji Kriol is a new language which comes from combining traditional Gurindji and Kriol. Kriol is a new First Nations language spoken across northern Australia. It looks a bit like English because most of its words are from English, but it sounds different and many of the words have different meanings. The map on page 2 roughly shows the areas where the three languages are spoken.

Violet Wadrill, Felicity Meakins and Topsy Dodd Ngarnjal working on the story in Gurindji.

Karu kamparnup

Although Gurindji children grow up in a world that changes all the time, many Gurindji traditions remain an important part of life. As you've learned in this book, tamarra (termite mound) and bush medicine plants are used to treat children, usually by their jaju (grandmother on the mother's side).

With more research we might better understand how the tamarra treatment works. Tamarra is full of minerals like iron, calcium, magnesium and zinc, which comes from termites collecting clay and soil to build their mounds. These minerals are important for humans, especially in early childhood. However, there might be other ingredients that we don't yet know about.

Rosemary Johnson, Joanne Stevens and Cecelia Edwards with baby Shirley Dodd, performing karu kamparnup.

THE TAMARRA PROJECT

The Tamarra: Gurindji Termite Project brought together ngumpin (First Nations) and kartiya (non-Indigenous) cultures. It was a collaboration between over 30 people, including Gurindji Elders, artists, storytellers and translators, together with kartiya artists, scientists and a linguist.

Led by Leah Leaman (Co-director, Karungkarni Art), we began the project by spending time together on Country, getting to know one another. We visited termite mounds, made art together and yarned over biscuits and cups of tea.

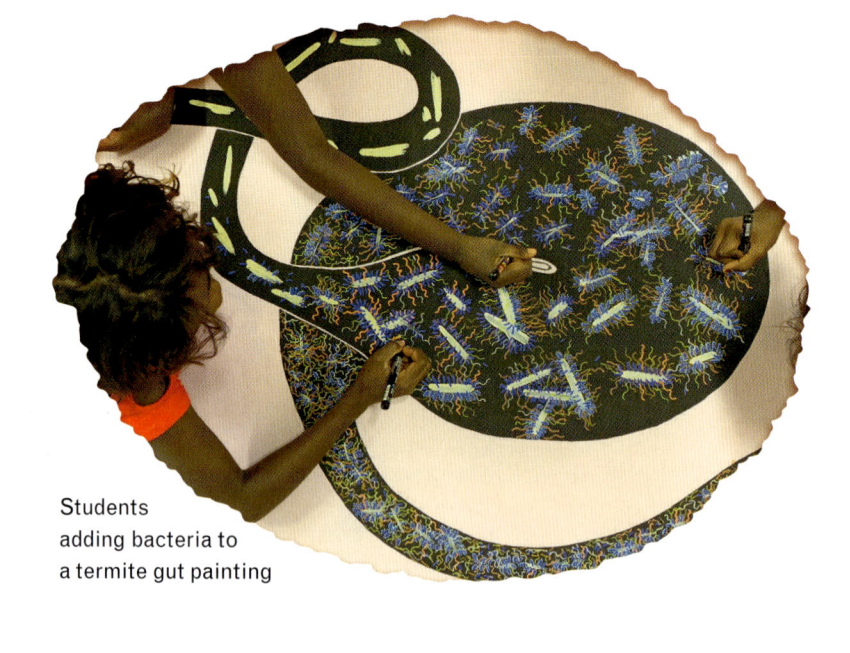

Students adding bacteria to a termite gut painting

Jacqui Young, Gregory Crocetti, Mary Smiler and Timmy Vincent visiting termite mounds.

Cecelia Edwards and Gregory Crocetti speaking about termites at Kalkaringi School

We held a large community meeting where Gurindji Elders, Violet Wadrill and Topsy Dodd Ngarnjal, and microbiologist Gregory Crocetti (Scale Free Network) talked about different ideas and experiences of termites and their mounds. We used three different languages (English, Gurindji and Gurindji Kriol), so Cecelia Edwards and Cassandra Algy (Karungkarni Art) and Felicity Meakins (University of Queensland) explained and translated to make sure we all understood each other.

Over the next months, we spent more time making videos of termites and their mounds. We collected samples of termites and spinifex, used microscopes to look at termites, gathered bush medicines and treated babies with termite mound.

All of us created the story. We worked on it bit by bit, adding and changing parts in English, Gurindji and Gurindji Kriol, until everyone's ideas were included.

Gurindji artists made paintings, both by themselves and with Briony Barr (Scale Free Network) and Penny Smith (manager, Karungkarni Art). One very large painting was made by 10 artists over two weeks (see pp. 80–81). The students at Kalkaringi School also collaborated on artworks.

Cecelia Edwards, Caroline Jimmy and Briony Barr collaborating on a painting of a termite mound.

Joanne Stevens, Lucy Tanami, Martina Mandijerry and Roberta Winbye collaborating on a large painting about karu kamparnup.

From left to right.
Top row: Briony Barr, Gregory Crocetti, Rosemary Johnson, Cecelia Edwards, Felicity Meakins.
Bottom row: Lucy Tanami, Violet Wadrill, Leah Leaman, Topsy Dodd Ngarnjal, Cassandra Algy.

Thank you to the many people and organisations who contributed to, consulted on and supported the development of this book:

The Traditional Owners of Gurindji Country

Kalkaringi School Community
Erika Charola
Anne Saunders
Brenton Hobart
Jacqui Young
Stephanie Daniell
Ellie Simmons
Ben Kinder
Jan Thompson
Bruce Garnett

Fiona Walsh
Theo Evans
Philip Hugenholtz
Glenn Wightman
Peter Jacklyn
Stephanie Johnson
Alan Andersen
Sarita Gálvez,
Bryan, Samuel and
Nahuel Phillips-Gálvez

Danae Moore
Joseph Schofield
Beth Sometimes
Sally Mumford
Watch This Space

Brenda Thornley
Jared Leadbetter
Mike Gillam
Susannah Tosh

Diane Lightfoot
Ailsa Wild
Aviva Reed
Alex Adsett
Thomas Mayo
Angela Foley
Ben Foley
Elaine Crocetti

Melissa Kayser
Amanda Louey
Irma Gold

scale free network art–science collaborative

THE UNIVERSITY OF QUEENSLAND AUSTRALIA

karungkarni ART

ARC CENTRE OF EXCELLENCE FOR THE DYNAMICS OF LANGUAGE

Australian Government
Australia Council for the Arts

Australian Government
National Indigenous Australians Agency

Australian Government
Indigenous Languages and Arts

Artists (pp. 9, 10, 13, 14, 80–81): Briony Barr, Merrilyn Frith, Caroline Jimmy, Martina Mandijerry, Penny Smith, Joanne Stevens, Lucy Tanami, Margaret Winbye, Magdalene Winbye and Roberta Winbye.